GARDENING
BY CUISINE

Italian Marinara

Three Sisters
Native American

Latin-Caribbean

Asian Stir-Fry

An Organic-Food Lover's Guide to Sustainable Living

GARDENING
BY CUISINE

Patti Moreno
THE GARDEN GIRL

rry, Berry Good

STERLING
New York

STERLING
New York

An Imprint of Sterling Publishing
387 Park Avenue South
New York, NY 10016

Images: Sydney Janey/SJ Design; Dover Publications, Inc.;
iStockphoto; Pepin Press; Shutterstock

ISBN 978-1-4027-9642-5

Distributed in Canada by Sterling Publishing
c/o Canadian Manda Group, 165 Dufferin Street
Toronto, Ontario, Canada M6K 3H6

For information about custom editions, special sales, and premium
and corporate purchases, please contact Sterling Special Sales at
800-805-5489 or specialsales@sterlingpublishing.com.

Manufactured in the United States of America

Book Design and Production: gonzalez defino, ny / gonzalezdefino.com

2 4 6 8 10 9 7 5 3 1

www.sterlingpublishing.com

*This book is dedicated
to my family for their love and support,
and for eating all their veggies.*

CONTENTS

INTRODUCTION

It all began in a garden...

How did I get into growing my own food? It started 70 pounds ago. That's how much I gained during my pregnancy in the 1990s. I was desperate to feel like myself again, and that's what led me into the garden.

❧

I am probably the least likely person to become a gardening and sustainable-living expert. I was raised in the concrete jungle of New York City in the 1970s and 1980s. I was clueless about plants and nature—I'd never even owned a pet. Unlike the generations before me—the baby boomers whose parents and grandparents had planted Victory Gardens to win the war—I had no tangible connection to food. As a Generation Xer, my memories of childhood meals go back to eateries like Mickey D's and classic, packaged comfort food like Stouffer's Mac and Cheese.

❧

After graduating, I married my college sweetheart, and we soon moved into our first house, a humble multi-level brownstone in Roxbury, Massachusetts. I remember telling my husband, after we saw the "for sale" sign, "If it has floors, let's buy it!" Well, it did have floors, and so we bought it. The house also came with a 4,000-square-foot lot. I remember looking at it, with its five-foot-tall city weeds, and feeling proud that we were landowners! I didn't know anything about gardening, but I knew I'd need a shovel and started digging. Before long I discovered what many urban gardeners soon find out: the stuff I thought was soil in my city lot was really bricks, stones, and broken glass. I could shovel only an inch down before a jarring shock blocked my way. I began to sort everything I found, including stacks of whole bricks and partial bricks, brownstone, pudding stone, and all manner of urban rubble.

❧

At that point, my gardening experience consisted of learning how to use a pickax and digging, which also gave me a great full-body workout. Slowly, the pounds began to disappear.

My horticultural breakthrough came about when I managed *not* to kill a set of dwarf apple trees. They survived the winter and suddenly started blossoming early the following spring. Low and behold, that summer I had fruit! The trees produced wonderful apples and plums, which I shared eagerly with everyone—and they were a big hit. It was a complete eureka moment for me: "I can take this tiny urban lot and grow my own delicious, organic food?!" From then on I was hooked.

For the next decade, I continued to evolve as a gardener, as I built on each success and began experimenting with different gardening techniques. In a new home, in the same neighborhood, but with much more land, I was able to take my vegetable gardening experiments to the next level and put everything I'd learned to the ultimate test: feeding my family produce that came *only* from the backyard for an entire growing season. I videotaped the whole process, made the videos available online, and produced a DVD series to share what I'd learned and to inspire people to live more sustainably.

Since 70 percent of the world's population will be living in cities within the next twenty years, according to the Population Reference Bureau, it is crucial that we all make it a priority to live sustainably in our everyday lives. Anyone can get started on the road to sustainable living by using organic methods to manage waste control and other natural processes, by conserving energy, recycling, planting trees, and creating more natural landscapes. Last but not least, living sustainably means eating locally grown food. One of the best ways to do that is to "garden by cuisine." If enough of us can grow a portion of our own food (including the ingredients to enjoy the cuisines we love best), this effort will have a real effect, not only on the health and well-being of our families, but also on our neighborhoods, communities, and the world.

HOW TO USE THIS BOOK

In *Gardening by Cuisine*, I want to bring my garden to you, to let you twist juicy tomatoes off the vine and serve them at your dinner table. If you are new to gardening for the kitchen table, you'll find great projects here, including step-by-step instructions. You may get your fingernails dirty, but you'll also get plenty of tasty kitchen treats for your family to enjoy in no time. If you've been growing your own food for years and want to learn a few tricks to save time and energy—so that you'll actually have the time to enjoy your garden—this book is for you too.

Part I covers the basics of cuisine gardening. Growing your own food isn't rocket science, and you don't need a degree in botany to grow healthy organic vegetables for pennies. Here, you'll learn all about building raised beds, where you'll be growing your food, including plans for building a 4'x4' raised bed and 4'x8' raised bed. To maximize the space you have, you may want to build a hoop house and a trellis, as well as other add-ons for your raised bed.

In Part II, you'll find plans for cuisine gardens, growing instructions, and recipes to take you through the entire growing season. You'll enjoy traditional dishes from around the world—including Italy, Asia, the Americas, and the Caribbean—all with a fresh, contemporary twist. Each raised bed, however, can give you so much more than just one meal. As your vegetables grow, you'll be able to use them individually, or combined with other veggies, to provide an assortment of classic, fresh, and organic dishes for your family. I'll also show you how to use traditional varieties of vegetables that grow well in small spaces (and taste delicious). In short, you'll learn everything you need to know to make growing your own food a reality. You *can* be a successful organic gardener using what you learn in this book. To boost your confidence, you can also view companion videos online at my website, GardenGirlTV.com.

If I can do it, you can too!

COMPANION VIDEOS

Still have questions? Visit my website at **GardenGirlTV.com** where I've posted free instructional videos to help you on your way to becoming a Cuisine Gardener. (See page 245 for a chapter by chapter list of videos.) In them I explain some of the trickier parts of home gardening, with the help of my gardening-expert friends (including my daughter).

Part I

CUISINE GARDENING BASICS

So you want to grow your own food. Congratulations! Welcome to the healthy world of gardening by cuisine. Beginners, don't worry, I'm going to talk you through it and be right by your side on your journey to self-sufficiency and food security. To be a happy cuisine gardener, you need to manage natural processes, so it's important to know the basics of what makes a successful food garden. Once you understand the natural processes that come into play when you are growing your own food and have learned the basics of cuisine gardening, it will be time to build your own raised beds and plant your cuisine gardens.

CHAPTER ONE

HOW DOES YOUR GARDEN GROW?

Gardens need three things to be productive: plenty of sunlight, nutrient-rich soil, and water. Without just one of these things, all you have is little more than a dirty weed patch. With all three elements, you have the beginning of a successful, healthy, and productive cuisine garden. It's just a matter of simple science and patient observation. Once you understand what's going on behind the scenes, you'll be able to create and maintain the ideal growing conditions for all kinds of delicious garden vegetables.

SUNLIGHT

Our sun is the most important giver of life on Earth. Since the beginning of time, the sun has been an object that we've feared, praised, and even worshipped. The sun provides light and warmth, and sunlight is an essential component of photosynthesis, the process through which plants convert energy from the sun into sugars that the plant then uses to grow. Some plants require little sunlight to grow, and others require not only a full day of sunlight but also many days of sunlight and warmth in a row in order to grow. Cuisine gardens require full sun and warm weather, which means at least six to eight hours of direct sunlight per day. Picking a sunny spot for your garden is key to growing plants successfully.

There are areas around your home that will receive more light than others during the summer (the peak of the growing season), while other areas may be in full shade. The place that usually receives the most sunlight is the south-facing side of your home. Most of us work during the daylight hours and may not even know where the sun shines the longest as it follows its path across the sky throughout the day. In the afternoon, for example, trees might obstruct a perfectly good south-facing spot that looks sunny when you leave for work in the morning, leaving you befuddled later on when your tomatoes and peppers do poorly. Shadows might even occur intermittently in the city or in an area where buildings are close together and block out the sun. Before you make a decision about where to plant your cuisine gardens, pick several spots that you have determined get plenty of sunlight.

SUN EXPOSURE & HOURS OF SUNLIGHT PER DAY

Full sun	6 or more hours of sunlight per day
Partial sun/partial shade	3–6 hours of sunlight per day
Full shade	Fewer than 3 hours of sunlight per day

Testing Your Sunlight

To accurately determine the sunlight around your home, you can use a number of low-cost products. One of my favorites is the Sunstick®, a simple, accurate test that you can buy online at www.plumstone. com. The Sunstick uses a photo emulsion film that "develops" based on how much sunlight it is exposed to. After you've assembled the Sunstick, position it in the ground where you want to test the sunlight; place it there before 9:00 A.M., and leave it outside for at least eight hours. Then match the color at the center of the emulsion to the chart provided in the package—that is the amount of sunlight that area receives. You'll be able to grow a cuisine garden wherever you get a "full sun" reading.

WATER

Plants grow best with rainwater. It's the right temperature and doesn't contain chlorine or other chemicals that are sometimes used to treat municipal water supplies. Besides, Mother Nature gives us rain for free. All you have to do is collect and store it for use in the garden on days when it doesn't rain. If you have a roof and a gutter, you can install a rain barrel. This is a great system no matter how many raised beds you have.

Cuisine gardens need to be watered deeply two to three times a week, depending on rainfall. An average of 1 inch of rainfall per week is sufficient. If the natural precipitation falls short of that, the garden needs water. Globally there are water shortages, and water is becoming more expensive to buy, so developing and using methods to collect, store, and conserve water is one of the most important things you can do to create a self-sufficient and sustainable garden.

Picking & Installing the Right Rain Barrel

There are a lot of rain barrels on the market. Here are some reliable tips for picking a rain barrel that will work for you:

Research the going rate for rain barrels, then determine how much you are willing to spend. It is also important to consider what will look good next to your home; you don't want your rain barrel to be an eyesore.

Buy the largest rain barrel you can afford so that the collected water will last a long time, even through a drought. If possible, purchase one at your local garden center or non-profit building-materials resource center. Look for a barrel that uses recycled materials. Installing your own rain barrel can be intimidating, but anyone can do it. Rain barrels work best with a hose for hand watering or filling up a watering can. The best place to install a rain barrel is at a downspout attached to the gutter closest to your garden.

Make sure the barrel is level, and place it as far above the ground as possible; that way you will have good gravitational pressure for the hose. An easy way to do this is to place the rain barrel on a large flat paver and then elevate it on cinderblocks.

You will then need to install a downspout diverter to direct the water from the downspout into the barrel. Once the barrel is full, an automatic overflow control directs the water back to the downspout. You can then attach a hose to the rain barrel and water your cuisine garden effortlessly.

If you're a really ambitious sustainable gardener, you can attach multiple rain barrels in a chain, and have lots of water to use for your cuisine garden and landscape plants.

A surprisingly large amount of rainwater can be collected from the roof. You can get 623 gallons of water per 1,000 square feet of roof surface per inch of rainfall. With those numbers, a light rain may fill your rain barrel, depending on its size. Use the rainwater often, and try to make sure that it is empty before every rain so that you can continue to water your garden for free.

Measuring Rainfall

A great way to save time *and* water is to know how much water your plants are actually getting from rainfall in your area. A garden needs at least 1 inch of water per week in order to grow well. If you know you're getting that amount from rainfall, you won't have to do any additional watering. To find this information, you can of course check the weather online, but reports aren't always accurate about conditions in your specific area. To measure the rainfall in your garden, you can purchase a rain gauge or make one yourself.

WHAT YOU NEED

- One 1-gal. jar without a lid
- Ruler

How to Make a Rain Gauge

Put the jar outside in an open area in your garden. After it rains, use a ruler to measure the amount of water, then record the date and the amount. Empty the jar and put it back in the garden. You can record how much water is in the jar daily or after a rain. Totaling the amount of rainfall for seven consecutive days will tell you how much rainfall your garden has received during the week. If your garden has received at least 1 inch of rain in a week, no additional watering is necessary; if it gets less than 1 inch of rain for the week, you'll need to water your garden deeply.

WHAT YOU NEED

- Outdoor frost-free spigot
- Drip irrigation kit
- 1 roll of 1-in. main-line tubing
- Solid ¼-in. tubing
- ¼-in. drip-line tubing

Using Drip Irrigation

Drip irrigation, a system originally developed in desert regions, is far more efficient than spraying or using a sprinkler system to get water where your plants really need it, at the roots. The best part about using drip irrigation is that you can use a timer—a convenience that reduces the time you'll need to spend maintaining your garden to just minutes a day. Anyone can install a drip irrigation system. It may sound technical and complicated, but it isn't.

The first thing you need is a pressurized water source. You will not be able to hook your drip irrigation system up to a rain barrel because drip irrigation systems require more pressure than gravity provides. To use a rain barrel as your source of water for drip irrigation, you need to use a water pump to achieve the right amount of pressure.

INSTALLING A SPIGOT

To be efficient, you—or, more likely, a plumber—will need to install a spigot near your garden that connects to your water pipes. If you live in a climate where the temperature falls below freezing, make sure that the spigot is frost-free; this feature will prevent the spigot from cracking in the winter and leaking after a thaw.

HOW TO USE YOUR DRIP IRRIGATION KIT

Once the spigot is in place, you will need to purchase a drip irrigation kit. The kit will contain a manifold (the name of the piece that connects to the spigot), a filter, a pressure gauge, and a battery- or solar-powered timer. You will also need to purchase a roll of 1-inch main-line tubing, solid ¼-inch tubing, and ¼-inch drip-line tubing.

GETTING YOUR DRIP IRRIGATION SYSTEM UP & RUNNING

1. Set up your manifold and attach it to the spigot.

2. Run the 1-inch main-line tubing all the way around your garden. You will be running the drip line off your main-line tubing, so it's a good idea to install the main line anywhere you think you might need water in the future.

3. Once the line is run, you will need to cap it off at the end to keep water from flowing out of the main-line tubing.

4. Pierce a plastic tube connector by pushing the connector into the main-line tubing at the base of a raised bed.

5. Attach the connector to a piece of solid ¼-inch tubing, and extend the tubing up the side and over the top of the raised bed.

6. Attach a valve to the end of the solid tubing, which will allow you to turn the water on and off.

7. Attach the drip line to the valve, and run it alongside your plants at soil level.

8. Secure the line to the soil with U-shaped tie-downs, then plug up the end of that drip line, and continue adding more drip line to the rest of your garden.

9. Keep the length of each drip line less than 15 feet long because water pressure isn't likely to be strong enough to push the water through the drip line any farther than that.

10. Visit **dripworks.com** to purchase a drip irrigation kit.

The amount of tubing you need will depend on the size of your garden. Your main-line tubing should be long enough to reach from the spigot around your entire garden, wherever it needs watering. The solid ¼-inch tubing is used between the main line and the surface of a raised garden bed. Drip-line tubing comes with holes that are spaced at various distances. This tubing runs on top of the soil, next to the plants, and waters them via the holes.

When to Water Your Plants

Water your plants in the early morning, just after sunrise, when temperatures are coolest, thus allowing the water to be absorbed into the soil instead of evaporating in warm sunlight. Watering when it's hot outside and the sun is high in the sky can actually hurt your plants. Not only will much of the water evaporate instead of reaching the roots of your plants, but the water droplets can also magnify the heat of the sun and burn the leaves.

The timer function on your drip irrigation system will come in handy. With a timer, you don't need to get up at the crack of dawn to water your vegetable patch or lie in bed feeling guilty about not being out in the garden watering. Set your timer to water your garden at least every other day. Pay attention to the weekly rainfall in your area so you don't overwater. If it is a rainy week, turn off the system and restart it when it has stopped raining for twenty-four hours.

Container Gardens & Drip Irrigation

Container gardens are ideal for drip irrigation because they dry out much faster than raised beds and need to be watered more often. Pay special attention to your container garden during periods of drought and on days where the temperature is higher than 85 degrees. On these hot days, water early in the morning and in the evening, too.

No matter what watering system you use, check the soil between rains and waterings to see how it is holding the moisture. Here's a reliable test that garden pros use: Stick your finger 2 inches into the soil. If it's still moist below 2 inches, you don't have to water. If the soil is dry (and your plants are wilting), add more water.

SOIL

The health of your plants is directly dependent on the health of the soil they are growing in. Soil is alive with millions of microbes in every spoonful. Soil biology is a complicated web of life that constantly processes nutrients into forms that plant roots can absorb in conjunction with photosynthesis.

A good indication of a healthy soil system is the presence of earthworms. Worms thrive in soil that is well aerated, has a balanced pH (more on this a little later), and is rich in nutrients. As the worms burrow through the soil they leave small tunnels and pockets where water can flow freely to the roots, enabling them to drain properly.

Another indicator of healthy soil is texture. With a hand trowel, dig at least 2 inches into the ground. If the soil in the scoop forms a clump, you have good soil. If the clump falls apart easily and crumbles, that means the soil could use more organic matter in the form of compost. If the clump sticks together like clay, that's also an indicator that the soil requires compost. The key to healthy soil is supplementing it with compost.

Compost

Compost is made up of decomposed plant matter and other biodegradable materials that can be used to feed your plants. You can purchase compost by the bag or truckload, or make it yourself, as I do. Making your own compost is a great way to reduce your impact on the environment; it cuts down on the amount of waste that goes into our landfills and is economical as well, since it provides free, nutrient-rich food for your plants.

There are so many things at your fingertips that you can compost, starting with kitchen scraps. Instead of tossing them into the garbage can, keep a small covered pail in the kitchen to collect the scraps. Toss them into your compost bin when the pail is full.

If you live in a city or suburb you probably put out grass clippings, leaves, and other general yard waste, along with household and kitchen waste, on the curb to be collected by the trash man. This strikes me as a case of wasted resources. You could be using this valuable compost to feed the plants in your landscape. Compost also helps retain moisture in the soil, saving you time and water.

WHAT YOU CAN & CANNOT COMPOST

What to compost: Grass clippings, shredded leaves, pine needles, wood ashes, sawdust, houseplant trimmings, hair, shredded cardboard, shredded newspaper, wooden toothpicks, paper towels, paper napkins, tissues, coffee grounds and coffee filters, tea bags and grounds (remove metal staple), cotton swabs, greeting-card envelopes, junk mail, shredded brown paper bags, cardboard toilet-paper and paper-towel rolls, wine corks broken into pieces, cardboard egg cartons, cardboard pizza boxes, and takeout containers.

What not to compost: Pieces of wood or large twigs (unless chipped or broken up into small pieces), diseased plants, rocks, gravel, bricks, rubble, coal ash, oil, meat, fish, bones, cheeses, cooked or baked foods, dairy products, cat or dog excrement, cat litter, human waste, disposable diapers, all plastics, and paper with a wax or gloss on it.

WHAT YOU NEED

- One 4' x 5' roll of ½-in. hardware cloth (a coarse weave of steel wire) or chicken wire

How to Make a Simple Compost Bin

Compost is basically a huge heap of biodegradable material, and it just isn't pretty. If you use hardware cloth or chicken wire, however, you can contain compost in an outdoor bin while still providing it with the airflow and moisture needed for the decomposition process. It's easy and inexpensive to make a bin (you can make one yourself for about $25) and start composting at any time of the year.

MAKING A SIMPLE COMPOST BIN

1. Unroll the hardware cloth (or chicken wire), saving the wire that comes with it.

2. Connect the ends of the hardware cloth using the enclosed wire to make a cylinder.

3. Place the wire cylinder where you want to do your composting.

4. Fill the wire cylinder with grass clippings, leaves, and anything else that is compostable (see box above). The key to making good compost quickly is to break the biodegradable material into small pieces as you put it into the bin. (It's the same concept as chewing your food well for proper digestion.) Continue to add material to the cylinder until it is full. As time goes by, the waste will compact farther and farther down in the cylinder.

5. Your compost needs water, so during periods of drought, water it thoroughly.

6. Continue to fill your compost cylinder until winter. Then let it sit until springtime. Make sure it contains a balance of brown matter—that is, such carbon-rich material as dried leaves, paper products, and wood clippings, etc., along with such green matter (nitrogen-rich materials) as grass clippings and kitchen scraps. This mixture will help your compost heat up and decompose efficiently.

7. In late spring, lift the wire cylinder from the compost pile and place it nearby—wherever you want to continue making compost. The good stuff that you want to use in your garden will be toward the bottom of the compacted pile. Peel off layers of material that is not fully composted with a shovel or digging fork and put it back into the repositioned cylinder.

8. Collect the rich compost from the bottom of the pile and use it to feed your garden. When planting new plants, add a handful of compost per seedling.

9. In the spring, use compost as "top dressing" for already established plants. At the start of the growing season, mix it into the garden soil as a nutrient-rich organic fertilizer.

If you have a large yard, you can make a bigger wire bin using a 25'x 4' roll of hardware cloth (or chicken wire). You'll need to use metal tie-downs to keep it in place as you fill it. .

How to Make a Worm Bin

A worm bin is the perfect micro-scale composting solution for anyone with a small patio or balcony garden. It also works well for condo associations, which can have regulations against the use of outdoor compost bins. In a worm bin, worm castings (or worm "poo") make a terrific natural fertilizer. As the worms multiply, you can also add them to your garden soil.

WHAT YOU NEED

- 1 plastic storage container (a solid color, not clear)
- 2 lids (one that fits tight on top, plus a larger one for the container to sit in)
- Screw gun with ¼-in. drill bit
- Newspaper
- Red wiggler worms (purchase these online or at a garden center)
- Coco fiber (see page 23)
- Squirt or spray bottle with water
- Kitchen scraps
- Cardboard
- Garden soil

To make a worm bin, you'll need an opaque plastic container. Buy one with a lid, but you'll also need a second lid (larger than the top one) to use under the container, for any fluid that seeps out of the holes you'll make in the bottom.

A properly aerated and balanced bin won't stink. If your bin gets smelly, however, it simply needs more carbon-rich "brown" material, such as leaves, hay, or dog fur, and less "green" material, such as kitchen scraps and the like.

In ideal conditions, a powerful worm bin can digest half its weight every day in kitchen and other household scraps. So, for example, if you have 5 pounds of worms in your bin, they will process 5 pounds of waste every two days. The more worms in your bin, the more they can consume and turn into potent worm castings.

1. Using the screw gun, make ten ¼-inch drainage holes in the bottom of the plastic container.

2. Make six or more ¼-inch holes around the sides of the container, 1 inch from the top, for air circulation.

3. Place one lid under the container to collect liquid, and line the inside bottom of the container with a piece of cardboard to keep the worms and waste in. (Any liquid will seep through the cardboard and drain out the bottom of the container, to be captured by the lid underneath the container.)

4. Fill the container with shredded newspaper.

5. Cover the newspaper with decompressed wet coco fiber.

6. Add water, little by little, with a spray bottle to moisten the contents. The newspaper should be moist, not drenched.

7. Add 1 pound of red wiggler worms. (Other types of earthworms will not survive in the worm bin.) One pound of red wigglers will consume half a pound of waste per day.

8. Add a cup of kitchen scraps to the bin and cover it.

9. Add kitchen scraps and other household waste to the bin everyday (see "What to compost" and "What not to compost" on page 20).

10. Use the liquid that collects in the lid underneath the bin to feed your plants. Mix two parts water with one part worm juice to keep the moisture level in balance and water your plants with it.

11. Every time you add kitchen scraps to the bin also add dry shredded paper or cardboard. If the bin is too wet, you'll see the worms at the top of the bin when you remove the lid; to address this problem add dry shredded paper or cardboard to the bin and moisten it.

12. Red wigglers multiply quickly, doubling in numbers (not in weight but in numbers) every two months. As they multiply, add more kitchen scraps to the bin or relocate some of the worms outside in your cuisine garden.

13. After three months, stop adding scraps to the worm bin, and wait until practically everything has been consumed (but make sure the contents of the bin remain moist). Empty the bin onto a small tarp and separate the worm castings from the worms, a scoop at a time. You can then put the castings directly on the soil around the plants in your garden.

14. Move the red wigglers back into the worm bin and start the cycle again.

Coco Fiber This sustainable, renewable resource, is made from coconut fibers and can be used in the garden as a medium in which to start seeds. Coco fiber makes a perfect bottom layer for your worm bin; you can also use it as a great addition to your raised-bed garden for good drainage. I love coco fiber because it comes in lightweight, compressed packages the size of bricks. To use the fiber, soak the bricks in water. One brick can expand to 2 cubic feet of growing material— the same amount in which garden soil is packaged and sold at retail garden supply centers.

....

WHAT YOU NEED

....

- 2 cups of fresh compost or worm castings
- One 5-gal. bucket filled with water
- Aquarium aerator or large stick for mixing
- A coarsely woven cloth, such as burlap, to make the "tea bag"
- Watering can

Feeding Your Cuisine Garden with Compost Tea

Even if you can create only a small amount of compost or worm castings, you can make it go a really long way by "brewing" a batch of nutritious tea.

1. To brew the tea, wrap 2 cups of compost or worm castings in the piece of burlap or other strong cloth. Secure the tea bag with a rubber band and soak it in a 5-gallon bucket of water.

2. Oxygenate the water in the bucket by pumping in air, using an aquarium aerator, or by mixing the water at regular intervals over a three-hour period. With aeration, the beneficial bacteria in the tea bag will start multiplying like crazy.

3. With a watering can, use the tea—right away—to feed your plants and infuse tired soil with a shot of powerful fertilizer.

4. For great results, repeat this treatment once a week when watering your container garden.

CLIMATE

It can be tricky to figure out the best time of the year and the number of days available for growing plants in your area, unless you know the *hardiness zone* you live in. Your zone is determined by the average range of low temperatures in your area and the kind of plants that will survive those low temperatures and grow again the following spring. Hardiness zones, determined by the United States Department of Agriculture (USDA), were standardized in 1960. The continental United States comprises zones ranging from Zone 2, the country's northernmost and coldest climate, to Zone 10, the southernmost and warmest climate.

How to Find Your Hardiness Zone

On the Hardiness Zones and Growing Seasons chart on pages 26–27, determine your zone by finding the locality nearest to you. Hardiness zones vary from state to state and from one geographical region to another. Once you know your hardiness zone, refer to the Average Last (Spring) and First (Fall) Frost Dates chart (below) to find your frost dates.

Sticking with plants that work well in your zone will ensure maximum growing success. For example, many fruit trees, including pear trees, go dormant in the winter and need a certain number of cold days (low temperatures) to continue to produce fruit every year throughout their lifetime.

Determining Frost Dates

The Average Last (Spring) and First (Fall) Frost Dates chart shows frost dates and the average number of days in the growing season for each hardiness zone. This information is important because it determines when you can start planting a garden and when the growing season ends. If you don't see your city listed in the Hardiness Zones and Growing Seasons chart on pages 26–27, consult the USDA map at planthardiness.ars.usda.gov to find your hardiness zone, then refer to the chart below to find your frost dates.

AVERAGE LAST (SPRING) & FIRST (FALL) FROST DATES

HARDINESS ZONE	AVERAGE LAST (SPRING) FROST DATE (+/- 15 days)	AVERAGE FIRST (FALL) FROST DATE (+/- 15 days)	AVERAGE # OF DAYS BELOW FREEZING	AVERAGE # OF DAYS ABOVE FREEZING
3	May 15	September 15	242 days	123 days
4	May 15	September 15	242 days	123 days
5	April 15	October 15	182 days	183 days
6	April 15	October 15	182 days	183 days
7	April 15	October 15	182 days	183 days
8	March 15	November 15	120 days	245 days
9	February 15	December 15	61 days	304 days
10*	January 31	December 15	46 days	319 days

* There is typically not a frost in zone 10.

Courtesy USDA.

HARDINESS ZONES & GROWING SEASONS

STATE	CITY	HARDINESS ZONE	AVERAGE LAST (SPRING) FROST DATE	AVERAGE FIRST (FALL) FROST DATE	DAYS IN GROWING SEASON
Alabama	Birmingham	7	Apr 2	Nov 9	220
	Mobile	8	Feb 28	Nov 29	273
Arizona	Flagstaff	5	Jun 9	Sept 22	104
	Phoenix/Scottsdale	9	Jan 19	Dec 18	324
Arkansas	Little Rock	7 or 8	Mar 22	Nov 12	234
California	Los Angeles	10	*	*	*
	San Diego	10	*	*	*
	San Francisco/Oakland	10	*	*	*
	San Jose	9	Jan 11	Dec 26	358
Colorado	Colorado Springs	5	May 4	Oct 3	151
	Denver	6	Apr 30	Oct 4	157
Connecticut	Hartford	6	Apr 26	Oct 9	166
Delaware	Wilmington	7	Apr 10	Oct 30	202
Florida	Jacksonville	9	Feb 26	Dec 3	279
	Miami	10	*	*	*
	Tampa	9	Jan 28	Jan 3	338
Georgia	Atlanta	7	Mar 24	Nov 16	236
	Savannah	8	Mar 1	Nov 25	268
Idaho	Boise	6	May 10	Oct 6	147
Illinois	Chicago	5 or 6	Apr 20	Oct 24	187
Indiana	Indianapolis	5 or 6	Apr 17	Oct 16	181
Iowa	Des Moines	5	Apr 20	Oct 12	174
Kansas	Wichita	6	Apr 12	Oct 26	196
Kentucky	Lexington	6	Apr 15	Oct 25	192
Louisiana	New Orleans	9	Feb 12	Dec 11	300
Maine	Portland	5	May 2	Oct 6	156
Maryland	Baltimore	7	Apr 11	Oct 29	200
Massachusetts	Boston	6	Apr 7	Nov 7	213
	Springfield/Worcester	6	Apr 26	Oct 14	170
Michigan	Detroit	6	Apr 26	Oct 17	174
Minnesota	Minneapolis/St. Paul	4	Apr 30	Oct 5	157
Mississippi	Jackson	8	Mar 23	Nov 9	230
Missouri	Kansas City	6	Apr 7	Oct 28	203
	St Louis	6	Apr 7	Oct 29	204
Montana	Billings	4	May 4	Oct 1	149

STATE	CITY	HARDINESS ZONE	AVERAGE LAST (SPRING) FROST DATE	AVERAGE FIRST (FALL) FROST DATE	DAYS IN GROWING SEASON
Nebraska	Omaha	5	Apr 25	Oct 7	164
Nevada	Las Vegas	8	Feb 16	Nov 27	283
New Hampshire	Manchester	5	May 11	Sept 26	137
	Portsmouth	6	May 13	Sept 24	133
New Jersey	Newark	7	Apr 3	Nov 7	217
New Mexico	Albuquerque	7	Apr 16	Oct 28	194
New York	New York City	7	Apr 1	Nov 15	227
North Carolina	Charlotte	7	Apr 11	Nov 9	224
	Raleigh/Durham	7 or 8	Apr 10	Oct 28	219
North Dakota	Bismarck	3	May 14	Sept 21	129
	Fargo	3	May 10	Sept 27	137
Ohio	Cleveland	6	Apr 13	Oct 23	192
	Cincinnati	6	Apr 13	Oct 23	192
Oklahoma	Oklahoma City	7	Apr 15	Oct 16	184
	Tulsa	7	Mar 27	Nov 7	225
Oregon	Portland	8 or 9	Mar 23	Nov 15	236
Pennsylvania	Philadelphia	7	Apr 6	Nov 4	212
	Pittsburgh	6	Apr 29	Oct 16	170
Rhode Island	Providence	6	Apr 16	Oct 22	190
South Carolina	Charleston	9	Mar 9	Nov 25	260
South Dakota	Rapid City	5	May 9	Sept 27	140
Tennessee	Memphis	7	Mar 22	Nov 13	235
	Nashville	6	Apr 6	Oct 28	204
Texas	Austin	8	Feb 17	Dec 6	291
	Dallas/ Fort Worth	8	Mar 3	Nov 25	267
	Houston	9	Feb 8	Dec 20	315
	San Antonio	8 or 9	Feb 28	Nov 25	270
Utah	Salt Lake City	7 or 8	Apr 19	Oct 25	189
Vermont	Burlington	5	May 8	Oct 3	147
	Rutland	5	May 13	Sept 28	138
Virginia	Richmond	7	Apr 6	Oct 30	206
Washington	Seattle	9	Mar 10	Nov 17	251
Washington D.C.		7	Mar 29	Nov 15	231
West Virginia	Charleston	6	Apr 22	Oct 21	182
Wisconsin	Madison	5	May 10	Oct 2	145
	Milwaukee	5	Apr 27	Oct 14	170
Wyoming	Cheyenne	4	May 12	Sept 26	137

* There is typically not a frost in zone 10.

CHAPTER TWO

CONTROLLING COMMON GARDEN PESTS & DISEASES

No garden is ever completely free of the pests and diseases that arise from year to year—that's just nature. Long spells of rain, for example, can have a disastrous impact on your garden. Slugs love moisture and can easily do a number on leafy greens after an extended rain. A rainy spell can also be ideal for fungal and bacterial diseases that can decimate your plants. A few years back, after twenty-one days of continuous rain in the Northeast, nearly all the tomato plants contracted a fungal disease and the first crop was wiped out. In this chapter I'll explain how to keep your garden healthy and what to look for so that you'll be quick on the draw when garden pests and other threats cross your path.

THE HEALTHY GARDEN

The best way to defend your garden and keep it healthy is to feed and water it well, treat problems as they arise, and rotate your plantings. Keep in mind that problems occur when conditions are ideal for niche organisms to infiltrate your garden.

Plant Rotation

Crop rotation is one of the oldest and most successful ways to keep a garden healthy. When you grow the same plants in the same place year after year, pests and fungi have a guaranteed food source. Insects can lay millions of eggs in the fall, and when they hatch and develop in the spring, their favorite food—your garden—will be right there for them. If you rotate the plants in your garden, however, hungry bugs will have to venture out and find their preferred source of food. Keep them guessing! A fungal disease can be hard to eradicate and can remain in the soil from year to year, and if you keep giving it a perfect habitat it will quickly destroy your garden.

Crop rotation also keeps soil from becoming depleted of nutrients. Corn, for example, sucks nitrogen out of the soil. If corn is grown for several years in the same spot, the soil will become void of nitrogen and ready to blow away in a cloud of dust. Beans, however, take nitrogen from the air and fix it into the soil through their roots. Alternating corn and beans helps keep soil healthy.

Healthy Soil

You are what you eat—that is true for both people and plants, and it's why soil quality and the use of compost are so important. Plants, worms, and microbes all feed on organic material in the soil. When you add organic matter to your garden often, you are providing food for the organisms that convert organic matter into the basic elements that plants can absorb and use for growth. Using compost (see page 19) as a mulch or top dressing helps soil retain moisture and provides the necessary food source for worms and beneficial microbes to do their job. Organically rich soil improves the taste of everything you grow. Factory tomatoes, which are fed a diet of processed petrol chemicals, are nearly tasteless compared to an organic heirloom tomato fresh from the garden.

Companion Planting

This book is dedicated to companion planting, not only because of the obvious culinary delights to be realized, but also because many plants thrive when they are planted with companions that attract beneficial insects and ward off pests. For example, we know that tomatoes and basil taste amazing when they're eaten together, but they also benefit from each other when they are planted together in the garden by keeping away aphids. You can relax as you read on, secure in the knowledge that the plans for the cuisine gardens in this book incorporate the principles of companion planting and group plants together in beneficial combinations.

Disease-Resistant Seeds

Before you buy any seed package for your garden, first read the label to be sure the variety you are buying is disease-resistant. Most seed packages give specifics about a variety's resistance to common diseases, and it only makes sense to try the hardy varieties first. Remember, gardeners who develop heirloom varieties are not saving seeds from sickly plants, only the healthiest ones. For generations, natural selection has guided passionate gardeners as they develop varieties that are great-tasting and resistant to common maladies as well. For the best results, check out heirloom seed catalogs and try varieties that have been developed for the climate you live in and the soil conditions in your garden.

Regular Checkups

Don't forget the obvious: Check your plants regularly. Remove any damaged or diseased part of a plant and discard it (do not compost it). A fungal disease, such as powdery mildew, should be treated with a fungicide right away before it overwhelms the garden. If such a disease is not treated immediately, there is nothing you can do once it takes over the plant or the soil. Remove any weeds that are growing in your garden because they compete for water and nutrients in the soil. They also provide shelter for harmful garden insects and a breeding ground for diseases.

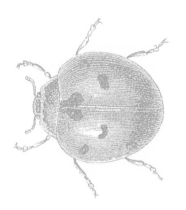

BENEFICIAL INSECTS

Attracting beneficial insects to your garden is a natural result of gardening by cuisine, which involves growing a diversity of plants. A healthy population of beneficial insects will keep your garden in balance. As you grow your cuisine gardens, look for good bugs such as honeybees, spiders, and ladybugs, whose presence keep away bad bugs like aphids, slugs, and caterpillars. If your plants have insect damage, you may need to deputize some beneficial insects and introduce them into your garden.

Ladybugs. These are the first "good bugs" that should be released in your garden. Ladybugs and their pupae feed on destructive aphids, consuming thousands of them during their life span. Be aware that many ants feed on the nectar of aphids and will go to war with ladybugs to defend them.

Green lacewings. The adult lacewing feeds on nectar and pollen produced by plants, but the larvae feed on aphids and nearly all soft-bodied pests such as caterpillars and inchworms. Green lacewings consume nearly 200 pests during their 15- to 20-day larval stage.

Ground beetles. There are lots of different types of ground beetles that don't fly and that instead stay in the soil, feeding on snails, caterpillars, slugs, and other bad guys that live in the dirt. You can spot ground beetles by their black shiny bodies. Don't go stompin' on these guys.

Beneficial nematodes. These tiny (microscopic), worm-like organisms do their magic below the soil line, eliminating more than two hundred species, including Japanese beetles, cucumber beetles, and other bad actors like grubs. You can easily introduce nematodes into your garden soil; they are completely benign in their effects on people, plants, and earthworms in your garden. But use them only when you have a problem; they don't have a preventive effect.

Parasitic wasps. These tiny wasps spend their nine-day-long lives seeking out the egg casings of pests in which to lay their own egg. The wasp egg consumes the pest egg as it develops into a tiny wasp, and the cycle continues.

Honeybees. These beneficial insects are key to pollinating the

flowers on your vegetable plants to help produce an abundant harvest. Honeybees fly from plant to plant, collecting nectar and pollen from the flowers. During this feeding process they leave behind pollen that results in the formation of fruit. I was blown away when I learned that 30 percent of the world's food crops need bees to produce various kinds of fruit—all melons, pumpkins and squash, cucumbers, and many more. Other plants, such as grains, whose seeds are produced from the flower without pollination, don't rely on bees for reproduction, but any plants that produce a fruit that contains seeds, such as apple and pear trees, are dependent on bees.

Currently, the population of bees in North America is at an all-time low; in 2006, beekeepers saw a large number of bees leave their hives, never to return. This exodus is called Colony Collapse Disorder. No one is quite sure why or how it happened, although a lot of research is being conducted to find out what the causes were. To do my part, I keep a hive in my garden, though it takes a while for a hive to become established and start producing honey.

Spiders. All spiders are a benefit to your garden because their webs trap all sorts of harmful insects that they like to eat. As far as I'm concerned spiders are welcome in my cuisine gardens.

For more information on beneficial insects and garden pests, visit Vegetable IPM (**http://vegipm.tamu.edu**), a website from Texas A&M University that has lots of images of common plant pests.

You can purchase beneficial insects online and have them shipped to you from a variety of companies. You can also buy them from your local nursery garden center or big box store. You can also try the following:

Arbico Organics
www.arbico-organics.com

Buglogical Control Systems
www.buglogical.com

Gardening Zone
www.gardeningzone.com

UNWELCOME GARDEN INSECTS

If your deputies—the good insects in your garden—can't keep pests out, do not fear. There's a lot you can do to get rid of them (see the Garden Pests and Natural and Organic Remedies chart on page 34). Here are some common garden criminals you may encounter:

Aphids. These tiny green insects feed on your plants in groups. They can blend in with your plants, so check them carefully. Luckily, ladybugs, lacewings, and parasitic wasps all feed on aphids; be sure to enlist these beneficial insects in your war on predatory bugs. Aphids can do a great deal of damage to your plants, so you need to treat them right away. You can also say bye-bye to these dreadful insects with a few applications of homemade insecticidal soap (see page 37).

Beetles. The damage from these really bad guys can be devastating—overnight! What makes them so dangerous as a group is their appetite for a wide variety of garden plants. For example, the potato beetle, which has a black-striped exoskeleton, likes potato plants. Iridescent black and brown Japanese beetles, on the other hand, love your grape plants. The aptly named cucumber beetle loves the plant it's named for, as well as your pumpkins and melons; these nasty bugs are yellow with either black stripes or black spots.

Slugs and snails. These creatures are really common, unfortunately, and you can see their path of destruction (large holes) on the leaves of your plants. They're easy to locate and capture, however, when it's moist in the garden or just after a rainstorm. Just check the underside of damaged leaves, pick off any slugs or snails, drop them in a bowl of soapy water where they will die and toss them in the garbage. There will probably be more slugs or snails in your garden than you can actually see, so try one of the remedies in the chart on page 34 to get rid of all of them.

GARDEN PESTS & NATURAL & ORGANIC REMEDIES

GARDEN PEST	BENEFICIAL ORGANISM	ORGANIC OR NATURAL TYREATMENT*
Aphids (tiny, green or black, soft-bodied insects)	Ladybugs, green lacewings; companion planting with marigolds	Homemade insecticidal soap, neem oil treatment (see page 37)
Caterpillars, cabbage worms, and **tomato hornworms** (long, soft-bodied insects, with multiple legs, that come in many colors and sizes)	Green lacewings, caterpillar parasites (*Trichogramma*); companion planting with nasturtiums	Bt (see page 36), neem oil treatment (see page 37)
Earwigs and **gnats** (have a hard exoskeleton with antenna and pincers)	Beneficial nematodes	Trap in castor oil or use homemade insecticidal soap (see page 37)
Mealybugs (look similar to aphids but have woollier "hair")	Ladybugs, green lacewings	Homemade insecticidal soap (see page 37)
Potato beetles and **Japanese beetles** (about half an inch long, with metallic exoskeletons and brown wings)	Ladybugs	Beneficial insects
Slugs and **snails.** (Slugs are soft-bodied blobs with antennae; snails look very similar to slugs, but have a shell)	Beneficial nematodes	Trap and remove slugs manually, trap them in beer, or treat them with DE or crushed eggshells (see page 36 for all three)
Spider mites (tiny pests that can be seen only with a microscope or magnifying lens, though it's easy to see their destruction on plant leaves)	Green lacewings, beneficial nematodes	Homemade insecticidal soap (see page 37)
White flies (tiny, white, winged insects found on the underside of leaves)	Green lacewings	Homemade insecticidal soap (see page 37)

*See other natural remedies on pages 35–39..

Spider mites. Because these pests are microscopic, you won't see the mites themselves, only the destruction they cause in the form of yellow-streaked patches on plant leaves. Remove the affected leaves and discard them. Treat the affected plant right away. (See the chart on the facing page for treatment methods.)

Caterpillars and worms. These creatures are a nuisance in the garden, where they attack a multitude of plants. Caterpillars and worms grow at lightning speed, so they have to eat a lot. If you see moths in your garden, you have caterpillars somewhere. Beneficial insects should balance out the problem, but you can try a few natural treatments. (See the chart on the facing page.)

ORGANIC NATURAL PESTICIDES

Animal barriers. Gardens sometimes attract animals—squirrels, raccoons, birds, rabbits, skunks, even deer. Putting up a physical barrier, such as 1-inch wire mesh, will deter wildlife like squirrels and birds. If you have a hoop house, you can put netting over it; rainwater will be able to get in and unwelcome critters will be kept out. Don't worry about putting up barriers right away unless you know that wildlife regularly passes through your area.

Animal repellents. You can also use chemical repellents to keep animals out of your garden. These can be purchased online and at your local garden center, but you need to know exactly what animal has become a nuisance before you purchase a repellant. Make sure that any repellent you buy can be safely used around vegetables, and be sure to follow the manufacturer's instructions.

Some store-bought repellents, such as hot-pepper spray (also known as capsaicin spray), can be very effective in deterring most mammals. A simple homemade brew of the peppery repellent can be concocted by chopping up a few blazing hot peppers and boiling them. You'll know the mixture is ready to spray in the garden when a taste of it is hot enough to burn your taste buds. Your plants will need a few treatments before your local furry friends are convinced that your garden tastes funny and they'd better go somewhere else for dinner.

BUY IT ONLINE

Here are a couple of places where you can buy animal repellents that are safe for your vegetable garden:

Liquid Fence www.liquidfence. com/natural-animal- repellents.html

Bobbex, Inc. www.bobbex.com

Bt (*Bacillus thuringiensis*). This biological insecticide is actually living bacteria that will kill many garden pests before they become a problem, from gypsy moths and caterpillars to tomato hornworms. It is also a safe solution for killing mosquito larvae in ponds. Apply Bt as soon as you purchase it, and check the recommended storage requirements and shelf life. Bt is a great option because it is completely safe for use around plants, animals, and many beneficial insects. You can purchase Bt spray or powder online or at your local garden center. The best time of day to apply Bt is in the evening or on an overcast day, since strong sunlight will kill Bt before it has a chance to be effective. Bt isn't an instant fix, however, since it takes time to infect and kill garden pests. Be sure to follow the instructions on the package when applying Bt.

Diatomaceous earth (DE). For out-of-control infestations of any common insect pest, you may need to take drastic measures, but you don't have to go nuclear. You can handle the problem organically by using diatomaceous earth, also known as DE, which comes in a fine powder composed of microscopic fossilized, hard-shelled algae. DE is perfectly safe for animal and human consumption (it's non-toxic), but use a mask over your nose and mouth when you are applying this fine powder in your garden to keep the dust out of your lungs. You can order DE online or find it at your local garden center. Before you apply DE it is important to water down your garden, including the leaves of the plants, because the water will help the dust to adhere to the leaves. Then, using a hand duster (a simple dust applicator that you can buy at your local garden store), coat the vegetable garden with the DE. Don't apply DE if it is going to rain within twenty-four hours. Re-apply DE after the next rain until all the pests are gone. Always read and follow the instructions on the package.

Eggshells and beer. Slugs are common garden pests that can attack a large number of plants. They are most active in the spring, when it's moist, and can eat up the leaves of your plants overnight. If you see holes in the leaves of your vegetable plants, slugs might be the culprits. When you notice the holes, inspect the leaves for slugs and pick them off and discard them. (I feed them to my chickens or the fish in my pond.) You can also get rid of your slug problem with beer. Pour as much beer as you can spare into a small bowl and bury the bowl so that its rim is at ground level. The slugs will be attracted to the beer and drown in it. One bowl per raised bed is fine. You can also get rid of slugs using eggshells. Simply crunch the shells into small bits and place them on the soil around the perimeter of your raised beds. Slugs won't like the way they feel and will retreat from the area.

Insecticidal soap. In an empty, clean, 1-liter spray bottle, combine 1 teaspoon of vegetable oil and 1 teaspoon of dishwashing liquid soap per cup of water. Spray the mixture liberally on any plant affected by a garden pest, thoroughly coating the leaves and stems. Wait an hour and then rinse off the plants with water to remove the mixture and any dead insects. Repeat this treatment three times per week until the problem is controlled.

Neem oil. Native to India, the neem is an evergreen tree whose fruit and trees produce a bright red, strong-smelling oil. You can buy neem oil online or at the garden center. It's safe for humans and mammals, and eliminates all kinds of harmful garden pests including aphids, mites, beetles, moth larvae, caterpillars, locusts, and nematodes. **Caution:** Neem oil is non-toxic, but should not be consumed by women who are pregnant or plan to become pregnant.

COMMON GARDEN DISEASES & REMEDIES

Garden diseases fall under a few categories: fungal, bacterial, and viral. Prevention is key to keeping these diseases out of the garden, and as you already know, prevention of problems is an integral part of gardening. One basic measure is to rotate your crops, varying where you put plants in your garden from year to year (see Plant Rotation on page 29). Despite your best efforts, however, insects, weeds, and transplants from other gardens can bring diseases into your garden. Unfortunately, there is nothing you can do when you spot a garden disease other than remove the affected plant.

BUY IT ONLINE

Many companies sell fungicides. Here are a few.

Bonide
www.bonide.com

Safer Brand
www.saferbrand.com

Natria by Bayer Advanced
www.bayeradvanced. com/natria

Common Vegetable Diseases & What They Look Like

There's more information on diseases in Part II (I give a list of diseases and remedies for each of the plants in every cuisine garden), but here's a brief introduction to some of the most common diseases so you'll know what to look for:

Powdery mildew. The leaves of your snap beans, cantaloupe, cucumber, pumpkin, and squash will have a white, powdery-looking dust on them. Once a plant has powdery mildew it's only a matter of time before it dies. Prune as many affected leaves as you can, and spray the leaves of your plant with an organic garden fungicide (see the section Natural Fungicides and Bactericides, below).

Leaf blight. Lower leaves turn yellow, then brown, and die as the leaf blight spreads to other leaves of the plant. Affects snap beans, corn, eggplants, peppers, potatoes, tomatoes.

Leaf spot. Brown to black spots on the leaves. Affects cantaloupes, kale, mustard, cucumbers, peppers, watermelons.

Stem blight. The stems near the soil yellow and die, killing the plant. Affects cantaloupes, cucumbers, pumpkins, watermelons.

Wilt. Leaves start shriveling up and die off, killing the plant. Affects cantaloupes, corn, cucumbers, tomatoes, watermelons.

Fruit rot. Brown spots form on fruit before it is ripe and harvestable. Affects eggplants, peppers, squash, tomatoes.

Natural Fungicides & Bactericides

Natural fungicides and bactericides, such as neem oil and copper, help prevent and keep garden diseases at bay. These come in the form of powders, granules, and foliar (leaf) sprays, which are used to prevent leaf spots, rusts, mildews, and fruit rot. You can use any of these remedies either before a disease hits or at the first sign of disease. Remember, once a garden disease takes hold of your plant, there is nothing you can do; the plant should be removed from the garden so that it doesn't spread disease to other plants.

DISEASE CONTROL ACTION PLAN

1. Look at your plants thoroughly and often. I like to do it when I water and when I harvest.

2. Along with a bowl or basket in which to gather the bounty from your cuisine garden, take along an empty container to collect weeds. It's good to get rid of weeds as soon as you see them because they can harbor diseases that damage the health of your vegetable plants.

3. While you're in the garden, ask yourself: Do the plants look healthy and green, and are they growing?

4. Remove any dead or yellowing leaves and branches because they can attract pests and diseases.

5. If you notice any of the diseases listed on page 38, remove the leaves and affected branches. Do not put them in your compost bin, however, because diseases can lie dormant in compost and pop up again in your garden when the conditions for their growth are right.

6. If you can identify a plant disease, treat it right away.

7. If there is no remedy for a particular plant disease, you may have to suffer through it and harvest what you can, or remove the entire plant from your garden. There's always next year . . .

CHAPTER THREE

STARTING YOUR CUISINE GARDEN FROM SEED

When you begin gardening by cuisine, you will start most of your plants from seed, right in the bed. However, many summer vegetables, like tomatoes, eggplants, and peppers, need to be planted in the garden from seedlings (young plants), so that there is enough time for them to mature and for you to get the maximum number of vegetables from them. Plants that require a long growing period—like tomatoes and many other summertime vegetables—are the ones you want to start indoors in the wintertime. Of course, you may opt to purchase seedlings from your local garden center, but by starting your own plants from seed indoors you can reduce the amount of money you spend on your garden to just pennies per plant. You can also get a jump on the growing season.

Garden centers carry a large variety of vegetable seedlings, but they are unlikely to carry the organic or heirloom varieties I like to grow in my cuisine gardens. Heirloom seeds are genetically diverse, are slightly harder to grow, and tend to have a lower germination rate than other hybrid seeds on the market, but the delicious vegetables they produce simply can't be found in grocery stores.

Organic vegetable seedlings can be really pricy, ranging from $5 to $10 per plant at most nurseries and garden centers. On the other hand, organic vegetable seeds cost, on average, $3 to $5 per packet, which, depending on the type of seed you are buying, contains between 10 and 1,000 seeds. The savings are clear, but what is most important to me is being able to actively garden when the snow is still on the ground.

CHOOSING THE RIGHT SEEDS

I live in New England, so I start seeds indoors every year beginning in February. I've started thousands of plants using many different methods. Every spring I sell or give away the excess seedlings to my friends and neighbors because I rarely end up using all of the plants for my own garden. The sales help me earn back the cost of starting the garden. To break even on other expenses, I also sell (and often give away) some of my produce to friends and neighbors. Sharing my garden with the community has been a great way to meet my neighbors and build new friendships.

I also buy plants every year from local nurseries and garden centers and even online. But purchasing all the plants I need every year would cost thousands of dollars, so I tend to limit my purchases to varieties of vegetables that I want to try for the first time. If I like the results, I purchase the seeds and start the plants myself the next year. Starting with the right seeds is very important. Here are some tips to start your cuisine garden right from the very beginning:

- Purchase seeds from an heirloom seed bank.
- Choose organic seeds.
- Pick seeds for plants that will grow well in your region.
- Order your seeds as early as you can because they sell out fast.

HEIRLOOM & ORGANIC MAIL-ORDER SEEDS & SEEDLINGS

Baker Creek Heirloom Seed Company
(seeds)
www.rareseeds.com

Botanical Interests (seeds)
www.botanicalinterests.com

Seeds of Change
(seeds and plants)
www.seedsofchange.com

Seed Savers Exchange
(seeds and plants)
www.seedsavers.org

Southern Exposure Seed Exchange
(seeds)
www.southernexposure.com

Stark Bro's Nurseries and Orchard Co.
(fruit trees, shrubs, and root crops)
www.starkbros.com

Sustainable Seed Co. (seeds)
www.sustainableseedco.com

Sweet Corn Organic Nursery
(seeds and plants)
www.sweetcornorganicnursery.com

- Grow-light fixture
- Timer for the light
- Daylight-balanced fluorescent bulbs for plants
- Light stand
- Heat mat
- Mini greenhouse (hothouse) with dome and tray
- Growing pellets
- Seeds

SEED-STARTING METHODS

Here are some of my favorite seed-starting methods. They require a bit of extra effort but are both cost effective and easy, and pay off.

Make Your Own Hothouse

A hothouse is a great way to start seeds indoors. It's a versatile system that includes a source of light, a heat mat, and a clear plastic dome.

Complete kits are available online or at gardening centers. The kit may include the growing medium for the seedlings in the form of growing pellets—coco fiber or peat moss compressed into flat disks. When you use this system, you want to plant seeds that germinate at roughly the same time and are similar types of plants. You can also start growing vegetable plants together, such as tomatoes and eggplants, when they have similar germination times and growth patterns. Once the seeds germinate and the plants outgrow the dome, you will need to replace the dome with a bigger one.

Mini greenhouses come in different sizes. The one that's best for you depends on how much you want to spend, how much room you have, and how many seedlings you want to start.

The grow light you use should be as long as your hothouse so that every plant receives the same amount of light. A heat mat regulates the temperature inside the hothouse, keeping it warm enough for the seeds to germinate.

If you buy a kit that has all or most of the items listed here, it will come with detailed instructions for setting it up. You can also view the video on my website: GardenGirlTV.com.

DIRECTIONS

1. Select your seeds.

2. Set up your grow light and mini greenhouse kit.

3. Pour warm water into the greenhouse tray with the growing pellets. I like to use pellets made out of coco fiber because it is a sustainable, renewable resource. Also, the coco fiber used in this application is a by-product of other manufacturing processes that make entry mats, hanging basket inserts, and other household and gardening items.

4. The pellets will expand as the water is absorbed. Pour off any excess water.

5. To plant seeds, place at least two seeds into the center of each growing pellet. This will ensure that at least one seed will germinate and become a viable plant. If both seeds sprout, you can either discard one or allow both seedlings to grow up to 4 inches tall, and then divide the seedlings before transplanting them in individual containers or into your garden bed.

6. Once all the pellets are planted, place the mini greenhouse dome over the seeded growing pellets.

7. Place the heat mat and greenhouse under the light stand and adjust the grow light so that it is directly above and almost flush with the dome.

8. Plug the heat mat into an electrical outlet. Use a timer to regulate how long the light will remain on. Plug the timer into an electrical outlet and then plug the light into the timer. Set the timer to turn the light on from 6:00 A.M. to 6:00 P.M.

9. The dome will help keep the environment around the seeds warm and the seeds moist.

10. The heat mat provides heat through the bottom of the greenhouse that is trapped by the dome, keeping the mini greenhouse warm. The moisture in the dome warms and evaporates into the air. This moist air then condenses at the top of the dome and drips down onto the seedlings, keeping the mini greenhouse environment moist for up to a week.

11. Check the greenhouse daily. Make sure the light is working properly and the pellets are moist. Water as necessary.

12. To prevent root rot once your seeds start to germinate, prop open the dome by leaning it on its side during the day; close it at night. This will dissipate some of the moisture, preventing your seedlings from rotting. Water only as necessary.

13. Once the plants are too big for the dome, remove it. Now you'll need to water the plants more frequently.

REUSE IT!

You can start seeds in containers made of different things found right in your home.

Coffee cans, metal and plastic (poke holes in the bottom for drainage)

Newspaper pots (see page 45)

Plastic takeout containers

Plastic water bottles (with the top cut off and drainage holes punched into the bottom)

14. Adjust the height of the light as the plants grow, keeping it 1 inch above the plants. If the light is farther away, the plants will grow toward the light, making them taller but weaker.

15. Once the seedlings are 4 inches tall, you can transplant them into containers filled with organic potting soil. There's no need to spend money buying small pots—you can make them yourself out of newspaper (see page 45).

16. Place the transplanted seedlings near a bright, sunny window and water them regularly. If you are not starting more seeds, you can also leave them under the light and on the heat mat.

17. A week before the seedlings can be safely planted outside, you'll need to "harden" them to acclimatize them to the outdoors. The young plants have been so warm and protected inside, it's a shock to them if you just plant them outside without getting them used to new temperature, wind, and sunlight conditions. To harden your seedlings, place them outside for an hour on the first day, then bring them back inside. The next day, increase the amount of time they spend outside to a solid eight hours. Your young plants are now hardened and ready to be planted in the garden.

WHAT YOU NEED

- Cardboard cores from toilet-paper or paper-towel rolls
- Large tray
- Coco fiber or seed-starting medium
- Seeds
- Water

Using Toilet-Paper Rolls for Seedlings

The cardboard cores of toilet-paper or paper-towel rolls are cost-effective, easy-to-use materials when you're starting seeds, and using them is a great way to keep these recyclable materials out of our landfills. Once I started saving toilet-paper rolls, I realized how much toilet paper my household uses. As a result, I don't know if we've actually cut down on the number of rolls we use, but we have switched over to using toilet paper with a high post-consumer waste content.

DIRECTIONS

1. Cut the cores of the toilet-paper/paper-towel rolls in halves/quarters to make tubular cardboard planters about 2 inches high.

2. Place the planters on a tray and fill them halfway with coco fiber or other seed-starting medium.

3. Water and refill the rolls with the seed-starting medium to the top of the rolls.

4. Sow 2 seeds per planter and water again.

5. Place the tray near a sunny window or under a grow light.

6. Keep the planters moist until the seeds germinate.

7. To prevent root rot, water the seedlings only every other day or when necessary.

8. Harden the seedlings as described on page 44.

How to Use Newspaper Pots for Seedlings

Once your seedlings are 4 to 6 inches tall, you'll need to transplant them to a larger container until it's time to plant them in the garden. Instead of buying pots, you can make your own using newspaper. Later you can even plant the seedlings in your garden, newspaper pot and all. This is a quick, easy project to do with your kids.

DIRECTIONS

1. Fold a sheet of newspaper lengthwise into a strip approximately 2½ inches wide.

2. Roll the newspaper strip around the can or jar, and tape it together using the paper tape.

3. Slide the newspaper strip about an inch off the bottom of the can or jar and fold it in to make the bottom of the pot. Tape it together.

4. Pull the can or jar out of the newspaper pot you just made and fill the pot with organic potting soil.

5. Transplant seedlings into the newspaper pot.

6. Grow your seedlings in the newspaper pot and "harden" them (see instructions on page 44) when it is time to plant. When you plant the seedlings, remove the newspaper pot, or just open the bottom and plant the whole thing in the ground, newspaper and all.

WHAT YOU NEED

- A stack of old newspapers
- Painter's tape (made of paper and used to tape walls before painting)
- 14- or 16-oz. can or jar
- Scissors
- Water
- Tray

WHAT TO PLANT IN LATE FALL

- Onions and chives, celery, peas, beans

- Leafy greens, including lettuces, Asian greens, spinach, kale, and chard

- Herbs like oregano, parsley, arugula, mint, sage, sorrel, and thyme

- Marigolds

WHAT YOU NEED

- Any small, used, shallow household container with a clear cover (for example, a take-out container)
- Compost, coco fiber, or other seed-starting medium
- Seeds

Sowing Seeds in Late Fall

A lot of gardening can be done in the late fall, when many gardeners are outside pruning, raking leaves, and putting their gardens to rest. In fact, fall is an ideal time to get a jump start on planting next year's crop by winter-sowing your seeds. Here's how: Just after the first fall frost, before the ground is frozen, and once you've put your cuisine garden to rest for the season, you can sow early-spring lettuce, herb, and vegetable seeds right where you want them to grow in your garden next year. There's no need to water the seeds or cover them with a hoop house (more on this in the following chapters). The seeds will simply sprout in the spring when the temperature and moisture are just right.

In Late Winter, Start Seeds in Flats

You don't have to grow seedlings indoors. In late winter, you can start them outside in flats at any time before the average last spring frost (see the table on pages 26–27 for this date in your area), then transplant the seedlings to the garden once they're at least 4 inches long. No hardening is necessary.

DIRECTIONS

1. Poke drainage holes in the bottom of the container.

2. Make 1-inch slits in the clear container cover for air flow.

3. Fill the bottom with the seed-starting medium you've chosen, and moisten it with water.

4. Sow the seeds in the container and cover it.

5. Set the container outside in full sun. The seeds will germinate in the spring.

6. Once the seedlings outgrow the covered container, remove the cover and allow the plants to grow at least 4 inches tall, watering them as necessary.

7. When the plants are 4 inches tall, transplant them to the garden.

Making & Planting Seed Tape

You can buy various types of seed tape, but it's really easy to make yourself. Seed tape is an effective way to prepare seeds for planting, and making it is a fun project to do over the winter with your kids.

Seed tape works best with vegetable seeds that are small and have a close spacing requirement, like radishes, carrots, lettuces, and herbs. Seed tape isn't necessary for sunflowers, corn, and beans because those seeds are large enough for you to easily plant with the appropriate spacing.

DIRECTIONS

1. To make the paste you'll use to attach the seeds to the tape, use your paintbrush to mix equal parts flour and water in a cup. Make sure the paste is thick enough to be sticky, not runny. It should stick to the paintbrush without dripping.

2. You can make your seed tape as long or as short as you like. Break off as many 4-inch toilet-paper sheets as you need. Cut the strip of toilet paper in half.

3. Read the instructions on your seed packet to find out what the seed spacing requirements are.

4. Lay a strip of seed tape next to a ruler. With a paintbrush, place a dot of paste at the correct intervals along the length of the strip.

5. Place 2 seeds on each paste dot.

6. Fold each seeded strip in half lengthwise, so that each seed is safe within the folded toilet paper. Press the strip down so that the paste holds the two sides of the paper together. Label each strip so you know which seed tapes are which.

7. Once the paste dries, roll or fold up the seed tapes and keep them in a cool, dry place until planting time. When it's time to plant, lay the seed tape in rows in your planting beds. Lightly cover each seed tape with soil, just enough to hide the tape, and then water it thoroughly. When the seeds germinate, they will already be perfectly spaced. The toilet paper will degrade in one season.

WHAT YOU NEED

- 1 or 2 tbsp. flour
- Water
- Roll of toilet paper
- Seed packet(s)
- Small kid's paintbrushes
- Scissors
- Ruler

GARDENING BY CUISINE ACTION PLAN

1. Determine the best location for your garden in a sunny spot that receives six to eight hours of sunlight per day and is close to the house.

2. Figure out how many raised beds you need or want to grow and how many raised beds you can fit in the designated area.

3. Decide which cuisine gardens you want to grow. Order seeds, seedlings, and other plants.

4. Start any seeds you need indoors over the winter.

5. Determine how you will water your garden. Add an outdoor spigot if necessary and/or rain barrels. Consider purchasing a drip irrigation kit for a low-maintenance, water-efficient system.

6. Start a compost bin.

7. Make sure you have all of the necessary building materials and gardening tools. Build your raised beds and, if you want, a hoop house (see Chapter Four for instructions).

8. Use a hoop house or flats to jump-start your garden until average nighttime temperatures are in the 60s. Fill the beds with a mixture of 50 percent topsoil and 50 percent compost.

9. Plant the garden according to the cuisine garden plans, starting with cool-weather crops and then summer crops, as weather dictates.

10. Keep seeds moist until they germinate, then water deeply two or three times per week.

11. Once the seedlings are 4 inches tall, weed, mulch, and water them.

12. Throughout the growing season, weed and water plants as necessary. Inspect plants often and thoroughly for pests and signs of disease and eliminate them right away (see Chapter Two for more on controlling common garden pests and diseases.

13. Harvest organic vegetables and herbs frequently so your plants will continue to produce.

14. In late summer, replant cool-weather crops for a fall harvest.

15. Continue harvesting the bounty from your cuisine gardens through the first frost or longer. Extend the growing season by placing hoop houses over your cuisine gardens when nighttime temperatures average 50 degrees before the average first frost date.

16. Before the average first frost date, harvest the last of the summer crops and can or freeze them for later use. Remove and store add-ons or support structures for use next spring.

CHAPTER FOUR

MEASURE TWICE, CUT ONCE: BUILDING YOUR CUISINE GARDEN

Building a raised bed doesn't have to be a costly, weeklong construction project—you can build a 4' x 8' raised bed in less than two hours for less than $70. Your super-efficient cuisine-garden beds should last between five to seven years. The whole proposition is easy, fast, and inexpensive.

For my raised beds I use dimensional pine lumber available at building-supply centers, but you can also use cedar, which will last longer but is much more expensive. After making raised beds out of all sorts of things, I've found that dimensional lumber, which is used to build houses, works best. I don't recommend using pressure-treated wood, however, because the chemical preservatives used in pressure treatment can be harmful.

There are so many ways to build raised beds. The plans in this chapter are designed so that you can make a raised bed all by yourself, but it's much more fun to build a raised bed with family, friends, and neighbors.

BEFORE YOU BUILD YOUR RAISED BEDS

Traditional gardening involves planting vegetables in large plots that require hours of work for a successful harvest. Your raised beds, on the other hand, will take only minutes a day to maintain.

Because your garden is off the ground and elevated by about a foot, it's easy to maintain year after year, without the backbreaking effort of maintaining traditional plots (most of which are only 6 inches high). All you have to worry about is the soil in your raised beds, making cuisine gardening super-efficient.

In a 4' x 4' raised bed you have 16 square feet of space to grow all kinds of vegetables. If you extend that bed to 4' x 8', you've doubled the amount of vegetables you can grow, but you haven't doubled the amount of time or money you will spend maintaining it. Weeding your garden will take just minutes a week because your vegetables will be planted close together, leaving less room for weeds to grow.

Although building materials like concrete blocks or stone are available for building raised garden beds, the best option is wood, since lumber is usually readily available. Although lumber will eventually rot, the advantages of its relatively low price and simple assembly far outweigh the longevity factor.

Great raised-bed kits are available commercially, but it's less expensive to build one yourself, even if you have to buy all the tools. Trust me when I say you can build your own for about half the price, even if you have no previous construction experience.

The best part of gardening by cuisine is that you can enjoy a continuous harvest throughout the growing season. When you "stagger-plant" your garden, you can enjoy leafy greens for lunch and fresh, steamed veggies for dinner. Each of the 4' x 4' garden beds you build and plant can be assigned to a family member—in fact, everyone in your family can grow his or her favorite cuisine garden.

Getting your family to "buy in" is really important to your overall success in gardening. As a result, they will enjoy the food they grow that much more and they will be more willing to help out because they are personally invested.

Once you get the hang of gardening by cuisine—say, in your second or third season—you can expand the number of cuisine gardens you plant and experiment with new ones.

CHOOSING THE RIGHT SPOT FOR YOUR CUISINE GARDEN

Locate your garden in a sunny spot near your home, preferably close to your kitchen door. It should receive at least six to eight hours of sunlight per day. Once you've chosen your spot, measure the area, draw it out on graph paper, and figure out how many 4' x 4' and/or 4' x 8' raised beds you can fit in the area, leaving at least 18 inches between the beds. Sticking with measurements that are a multiple of 4 feet will eliminate wasting lumber and save you money. When you buy wood at a building-material supply center, the standard length is 8 feet, which helps.

Using raised beds that are the same size will standardize and streamline your garden; the beds literally become the design building blocks you will plan around. The accessories you create, like hoop houses, planting grids, and trellises, will fit all the beds and be interchangeable between them.

PREPARING THE SOIL

To prepare the area for your raised beds, first remove any debris and pull up anything that may be growing there. Lay down at least a 2-inch-thick layer of ¾-inch gravel. If you like, before you lay down the gravel, you can first lay down a thick layer of newspaper as an additional weed block under the gravel. This newspaper layer isn't necessary, but the gravel is. The gravel provides proper drainage, kills most grass or weeds, and makes it easy to level the area. Proper drainage also keeps the raised bed intact much longer than if it were sitting directly on the soil.

MAKING YOUR RAISED BEDS

People build raised gardens out of all sorts of things, from recycled lumber to old tires.

I like using simple SPF (spruce, pine, fir) dimensional (building-grade) lumber because it is readily available. The thicker the lumber you use, the longer your raised bed will last. A raised bed made of

2-inch-thick dimensional pine lumber will last between five and seven years, which is the average time most people live in their homes. When you purchase lumber, most retailers offer a free cutting service, which eliminates a step and makes it easy to transport, even in a compact car.

I don't recommend using recycled wood because you can't be sure it has never been in contact with toxic fluids like paint, oils, or gasoline. Nor do I recommend using pressure-treated lumber, because arsenic was used in the past to pressure-treat wood. Although it is not legal now to use toxic chemicals to process wood intended for residential use, beware of using recycled pressure-treated wood. If you have the means, composite wood is a great option, and it lasts a lifetime.

These are the basic building and gardening tools you'll need:

- Small electric hand drill and screw bits
- Manual screwdriver with interchangeable bits
- Hammer
- Rubber mallet
- Metal clippers
- Small handsaw
- Pliers
- Shovel
- Digging fork
- Hand trowel

BUILDING A 4' x 8' FRAME FOR A RAISED BED

This chart shows everything you'll need to build a 4' x 8' raised bed for your cuisine garden:

ITEM	DESCRIPTION	AVERAGE PRICE
Hardware cloth*	One 4' x 8' piece of 19-gauge wire cloth with a ½" mesh	$68.00
Deck screws	1-lb. box of 3½" rust-proof screws	$9.37
Dimensional lumber	3 lengths of 2" x 10" x 8' wood (spruce, pine, fir, or cedar)	$23.34
Galvanized metal screw and washer set	Twelve 2"-long, ¼" screws, and twelve 1" washers	$10.00

*You'll have to buy a 25' roll of hardware cloth. You'll use the whole roll to make three 4' x 8' raised garden beds or six 4' x 4' beds. With any leftover cloth you can easily make a compost bin (see instructions on pages 20–21).

WHAT YOU NEED

- Wood, screws, washers, and hardware cloth (see chart on p. 53)
- Electric screw gun with a ¼-in. by 2-in. drill bit and a screwdriver set
- Safety goggles
- Gloves
- Metal snips

Finished Measurements

- 4 ft. x 8¼ ft. x 9½ in.

1. Cut one of the 8-foot lengths of lumber into two 4-foot-long pieces.

2. Measure ¾ inches from the end of each of the two 4-foot pieces of lumber, and draw a vertical line on the wood with a pencil. This is where you will pre-drill holes in order to assemble the four sides of the frame.

3. Next, mark where you will pre-drill the 3 holes along the line you've drawn. Draw one dot 1 inch from the top of the line, one dot in the middle, and one dot 1 inch from the bottom of the line.

4. Using a ¼-inch drill bit, pre-drill three holes where you've marked them.

5. Assemble a box from the lumber with the deck screws. Line up the pre-drilled holes on the 4-foot pieces of lumber with the ends of the 8-foot pieces of lumber, and attach the pieces using the 4-inch deck screws.

ATTACHING HARDWARE CLOTH

1. This step might be overkill, but I've found it helpful to keep animals from burrowing under the raised bed and destroying my plants.

2. Once the four-sided frame of the bed is assembled, roll out the hardware cloth, positioning it evenly across the sides of the frame to create the bottom or floor of the frame.

3. Attach the hardware cloth with the 2-inch galvanized metal screws and 2-inch washers, one on each corner and two in the middle of each board, for a total of 12 screws.

4. Trim away any extra hardware cloth.

5. Flip the frame right (open) side up and place it where you want to grow your garden.

ADDING A SECOND TIER TO YOUR 4' x 8' RAISED BED

WHAT YOU NEED

- Six 12 in.-long pieces of 2-in. x 4-in. wood
- Twelve 4-in. deck screws

Finished Measurements

- 4 ft. x 8¼ ft. x 19 in.

Making your raised bed higher by adding additional tiers is a great way to make it more accessible to anyone who is not able to bend over easily.

1. To add another tier to your raised bed, all you need to do is assemble another frame (without attaching hardware cloth), as directed above.

2. Position the lower tier of the raised bed (that is, the frame with hardware cloth attached to the bottom) where you want to grow the garden, then place the second tier on top of it.

3. Place one piece of 2-inch x 4-inch wood vertically in each corner and vertically in the center of each 8-foot side, flush with the bottom of the raised bed.

4. Attach the top and bottom tiers by screwing two screws into the 2-inch x 4-inch pieces of wood at an angle in line with the top tier and one in line with the bottom tier. Basically, you're going to secure the two tiers by using the pieces of 2-inch x 4-inch wood as braces between the two tiers. The screws need to go in at an angle for a longer-lasting, tighter fit. Also, putting the screws in at an angle ensures that they won't go all the way through the wood and out the other side.

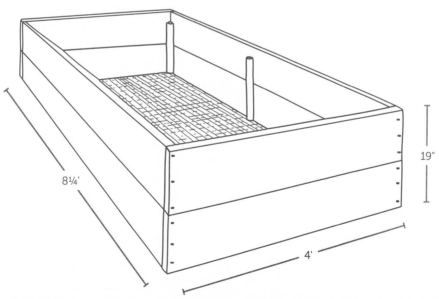

FILLING YOUR 4' x 8' RAISED BEDS WITH SOIL

To fill a single-tier raised bed you'll need 8 inches of soil, leaving enough room in the frame to add a 1-inch-thick layer of mulch. Altogether, you will need 22 cubic feet of soil to fill it 8 inches high. You'll need 44 cubic feet of soil for a two-tier bed.

In cuisine gardening, you have a chance to start out with the perfect soil mixture. I asked my friend Mark Highland, a soil scientist and owner of Organic Mechanics Potting Soil, to chime in on the best soil mixture for growing your own food in raised beds. Here's what he had to say:

> "When I talk to people about raised beds, I recommend a 50/50 blend of topsoil and compost. If they don't have access to topsoil (either no transportation or no funds), they certainly can go with less topsoil, but I always recommend at least 25 percent topsoil. Why? There is a synergy between sand, silt, clay, and the organic matter in compost that leads to more nutrients and water-retentive gardens."

To achieve the ideal soil mixture for a single-tier 4' x 8' raised bed, you'll need 11 cubic feet of topsoil and 11 cubic feet of compost. Fill the bed a little at a time with the topsoil and compost, mixing it together as you go. If you've built two tiers high, double the amount of soil and compost to 22 cubic feet of topsoil and 22 cubic feet of compost.

After filling the bed with the soil mixture, water it thoroughly. Now you're ready to plant.

If you are building a bed of different dimensions and want to calculate the cubic feet of soil you will need, multiply the length in feet times the width in feet times the height in feet of your raised bed (make sure all of these measurements are in feet). Because of the thickness of the boards and the extra inch or so of mulch at the top of the bed, the formula will yield slightly more soil than you need.

MAKING AN EASY PLANTING GRID FOR A 4' x 8' RAISED BED

Constructed from long, thin pieces of wood, a planting grid helps you space plants correctly in your raised beds so that you can maximize their growing space. I strongly suggest you make a grid for each of your cuisine gardens—or you can simply make one grid and move it from bed to bed as you plant each of them. A planting grid should fit inside a raised bed and rest on the soil.

Planting grids are easy to make using laths that are about 1 inch wide, ¼ inch thick, and 8 feet long. Make sure you measure the inside of your raised bed before you make a cut, and adjust the measurements provided below accordingly.

1. Clamp the three 8-foot wood laths together, making sure they are flush.

2. Using a measuring tape and a pencil, mark the wood at 1-foot intervals. There should be seven marks on the wood.

3. With a ³⁄₁₆-inch drill bit, drill a hole through each of the pencil marks on the three wood laths.

4. Clamp three of the shorter (45-inch) laths together, making sure they are flush to each other. Measure and mark the top piece of wood in the center, 22½ inches from the end. Then measure and mark the top piece 1 foot to the right and left of the center mark.

5. Drill holes through the clamped pieces at each of the pencil marks. Clamp together the remaining four shorter laths and repeat the measuring, marking and drilling process.

6. Lay the long laths on the ground about 12 inches apart, then lay the shorter pieces of lath across them at 1-foot intervals, lining up the drill holes.

7. Place screws in the drill holes and secure the laths with wing nuts. Tighten the wing nuts just enough for the laths to slide and collapse easily. Place the grid on top of the soil in the raised bed. Because these planting grids are attached with screws and wing nuts, they are easily collapsed and take up little space when stored.

WHAT YOU NEED

- 3 wood laths
  1 in. x ¼ in. x 8 ft.
- 7 wood laths
  1 in. x ¼ in. x 45 in.
- Electric drill and drill bit set
- 24 screws and wing nuts
- Handsaw or electric saw
- 2 clamps
- Pencil
- Measuring tape

Finished Measurements

- On the inside, most 4' x 8' raised beds measure 8 ft. long and 45 in. wide.

WHAT YOU NEED

- One 8-ft. length of ½-in. PVC pipe
- Five 6-ft. lengths of ½-in. PVC pipe
- Drill and ¼-in. x 1½-in. drill bit
- ¼-in. x 1½-in. screws and ¼-in. wing nuts
- Handsaw
- 9-ft. x 12-ft. piece of 3-mil-thick plastic sheeting

MAKING A HOOP HOUSE FOR A 4' x 8' BED

A hoop house creates a microclimate around your plants, keeping them warm and moist and growing. In the early, cooler days of spring, a hoop house can help jump-start your garden and extend the growing season into the winter, even after the average first fall frost. In hot climates, secure a shade cloth to the hoop house to give plants extra protection from the sun.

1. Drill a hole through the middle of each 6-foot piece of PVC pipe.

2. Drill a ¼-inch hole, 1 inch from each end of the 8-foot piece of pipe. Drill a hole in the middle of the pipe (at 4 feet), and drill another hole 2 feet from the center hole on either side of the pipe.

3. Now attach one shorter piece of pipe at every hole along the long piece of pipe, using the screws and wing nuts. The long piece of PVC pipe will form the center ridge of the hoop house; it should rest on top of the shorter pieces of pipe.

4. Gently bend the shorter pieces of PVC pipe and stick them into the soil on the inside of the raised bed.

5. Cover the frame you've just built with thick plastic sheeting and secure it to the frame.

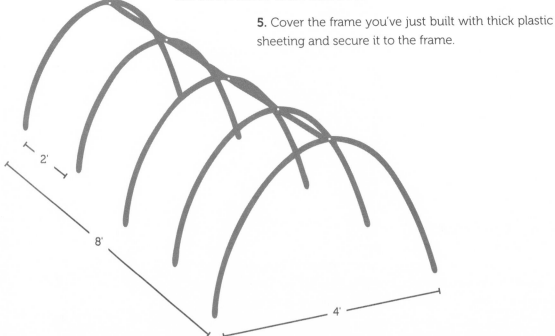

BUILDING A 4' x 4' FRAME FOR A RAISED BED

You can build a 4' x 4' raised bed in less than two hours for about $50. Here's everything you'll need and what it will cost.

ITEM	DESCRIPTION	AVERAGE PRICE
Hardware cloth*	One 4' x 4' piece of 19-gauge wire cloth with a ½" mesh	$18.00
Deck screws	1-lb. box of 3½"-long, rust-proof screws	$9.37
Dimensional lumber	4 lengths of 2" x 10" x 4' wood (spruce, pine, fir, or cedar)	$15.56
Screw and washer set	Eight 2"-long screws	$10.00

*You may have to buy a 25-foot roll of hardware cloth. You'll use the whole roll to make three 4' x 8' raised garden beds or six 4' x 4' beds. With any leftover cloth you can easily make a compost bin (see instructions on pages 20–25).

1. Measure ¾ inches from the end of each of two 4-foot pieces of lumber, and draw a vertical line on the wood with a pencil. This is where you will pre-drill holes in order to assemble the four sides of the frame.

2. Next, mark where you will pre-drill the 3 holes along the line you've drawn. Draw one dot 1 inch from the top of the line, one dot in the middle, and one dot 1 inch from the bottom of the line.

3. Using a ¼-inch drill bit, pre-drill the three holes you marked.

4. Assemble a box from the lumber with the deck screws. Line up the pre-drilled holes on the first two 4-foot pieces of lumber with the ends of the other 4-foot pieces of lumber, and attach the pieces using the 4-inch-long deck screws.

ATTACHING HARDWARE CLOTH

1. This step might be overkill, but I've found it helpful to keep animals from burrowing under the raised bed and destroying my plants.

2. Once the four-sided frame of the bed is assembled, roll out the hardware cloth, positioning it evenly across the sides of the frame to create the bottom of the frame.

WHAT YOU NEED

- Electric screw gun with drill bit and screwdriver set
- Safety goggles
- Gloves
- Metal snips

Finished Measurements

- 4 ft. x 4¼ ft. x 9½ in.

3. Attach the hardware cloth with the 2-inch washers and screws to each corner of the wooden bed and to the middle of each board.

4. Trim away any extra hardware cloth.

5. Flip the bed right (open) side up and place it where you want to grow your garden.

ADDING A SECOND TIER TO A 4' x 4' RAISED BED

Making your raised bed higher by adding an additional tier is a great way to make it more accessible to anyone who is not able to bend over easily. If you want a higher raised bed, build another bed—without attaching the hardware cloth—and follow these directions:

1. To add another tier to your raised bed, all you need to do is assemble another frame (without attaching hardware cloth).

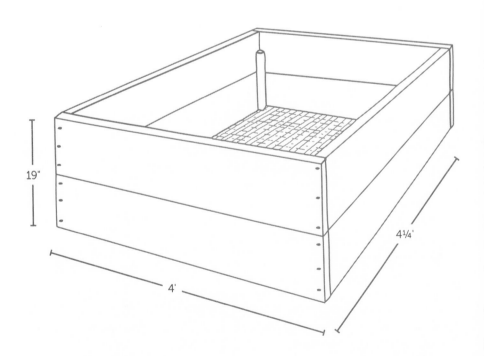

2. Position the lower tier of the raised bed (that is, the frame with hardware cloth attached to the bottom) where you want to grow the garden, then place the second tier on top of it.

3. Place one piece of 2-inch x 4-inch wood vertically in each corner and vertically in the center of each 8-foot side, flush with the bottom of the raised bed.

4. Attach the top and bottom tiers by screwing two screws into the 2-inch x 4-inch pieces of wood at an angle in line with the top tier and one in line with the bottom tier. Basically, you're going to secure the two ties by using the 2-inch x 4-inch pieces of wood as braces between the two tiers. The screws need to go in at an angle for a longer-lasting, tighter fit. Also, putting the screws in at an angle ensures that they won't go all the way through the wood and out the other side.

FILLING YOUR 4' x 4' RAISED BEDS WITH SOIL

To fill a single-tier raised bed you'll need 8 inches of soil, leaving enough room in the frame to add a 1-inch-thick layer of mulch. Altogether, you will need 10 cubic feet of topsoil and compost to fill it 8 inches high. You'll need 20 cubic feet of topsoil and compost for a two-tier bed.

For more on the composition of the soil mixture and how to calculate cubic feet for raised beds of different dimensions, see the section "Filling Your 4' x 8' Raised Bed with Soil" on page 56.

WHAT YOU NEED

For One Tier
- 5 cubic ft. of topsoil
- 5 cubic ft. of compost

For Two Tiers
- 10 cubic ft. of topsoil
- 10 cubic ft. of compost

WHAT YOU NEED

- 6 pieces of wood lath
  1 in. x ¼ in. x 48 in.
- Electric drill and
  drill bit set
- Screws and wing nuts
- Handsaw or electric
  saw
- Clamps
- Pencil
- Measuring tape

Finished
Measurements

- The inside
  measurement of a 4' x 4'
  raised bed is 48 in. long
  by 45 in. wide.

MAKING A PLANTING GRID FOR 4' x 4' RAISED BED

1. See the opening paragraphs of "Making an Easy Planting Grid . . ." on p. 57.

2. Clamp the three 48-inch pieces of wood together, making sure they are flush.

3. Using the measuring tape and pencil, mark the wood at 1-foot intervals. There should be three marks on the wood.

4. With a ³/₁₆-inch drill bit, drill a hole through the three pieces of wood at every 1-foot mark.

5. Clamp three of the shorter (45-inch) pieces of wood together, making sure they are flush, and place a mark centered on the wood at 22½ inches. Then mark 1 foot from the center on either side.

6. Drill holes through the pieces of wood at the marks.

7. Lay three of the pieces of wood on the ground about 9 inches apart, then lay the shorter pieces across them at 1-foot intervals, lining up the drill holes.

8. Place the screws in the drill holes and secure the laths with the wing nuts. Tighten the wing nuts. Because these planting grids are attached with screws and wing nuts, the grid can be easily collapsed and take up little space when stored.

9. When you are ready to plant, place the grid on top of the soil in a raised bed.

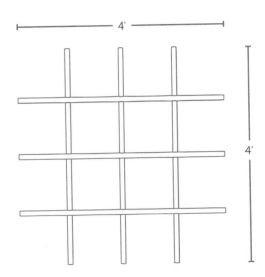

MAKING A HOOP HOUSE FOR A 4' x 4' RAISED BED

1. See "Making a Hoop House . . ." on page 58.

2. Drill a hole through the middle of each piece of PVC tubing.

3. Connect the two pieces with a screw and wing nut.

4. Gently bend the PVC as you insert the four ends of the tubing into the soil on the inside of the raised bed.

5. Cover the hoop frame with plastic sheeting and secure it to the tubing.

WHAT YOU NEED

- Two 6-ft. lengths of ½-in. PVC tubing
- Drill and drill bit
- Screws and wing nuts
- Handsaw
- 9-ft. x 12-ft. piece of 3-mil-thick plastic sheeting cut down to 9 ft. x 9 ft.

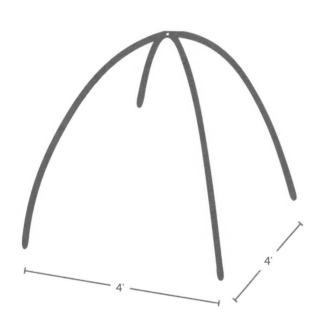

- Two 2-in. x 2-in. x 8-ft. strips of wood
- One 4-ft. x 25-ft. roll of 14-gauge welded wire, 2-in. x 4-in. mesh
- Six ¼-in. x 1-in. galvanized screws and 1-in.-wide washers
- Six ¼-in. x 3-in. galvanized screws

BUILDING A TRELLIS

A trellis is a structure that supports climbing plants such as cucumbers and melons, or plants that need support as they grow and produce fruit (such as tomatoes). The trellises I make out of scrap wood and welded wire for my garden can also be used to espalier fruit trees, a technique that keeps them supported, compact, and productive.

1. Cut the mesh so that it's 4 feet wide and 6 feet tall.

2. Using the washers and screws, attach the mesh flush with the end of the strips of wood, leaving 2 feet of wood along the bottom.

3. Screw the trellis to the outside of the raised bed with at least three galvanized screws per strip of wood.

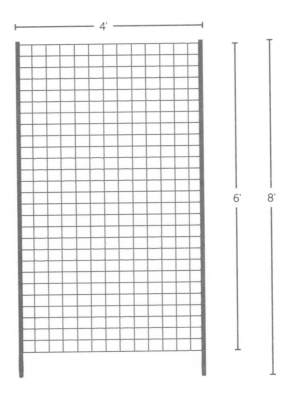

BUILDING A WINDOW BOX

This is an easy project to make out of wood, and it can be assembled using a finish nailer, a type of nail gun that is powered by an air compressor or a battery and a gas cartridge. You can purchase or rent a finish nailer from your local hardware store.

You can use this window box to plant a container version of many of the cuisine gardens in Part II.

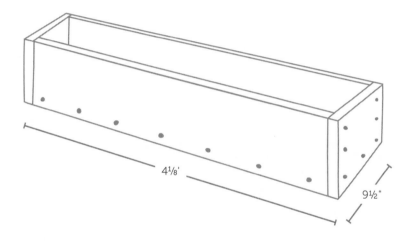

1. Drill eight ¼-inch holes in the middle of one of the 4-foot x 1-inch x 8-inch pieces of wood for drainage. This will be the bottom piece of the window box.

2. Lay the bottom piece flat on a work surface.

3. Line up the other two 4-foot pieces of wood (the front boards and back boards) flush with the outside edge of the bottom piece (not on top of the wood). Attach the wood with the finish nailer along the outside edge of the front and back pieces so that they're secure. Then attach the smaller side pieces by laying them flush with the bottom pieces of wood and the front and back pieces. Secure them with the finish nailer.

4. Attach a 4-foot piece of 2-inch x 4-inch wood, centered under the window where you want to put the window box, using decking screws (for wooden walls) or masonry screws (for brick walls).

5. Center the window box flush to the piece of 2-inch x 4-inch wood under your window, and use at least 4 deck screws to attach it to the wall through the back board of the window box and the 2-inch x 4-inch piece you've fastened to the wall of the house.

6. Now prepare the window box for planting by filling the bottom inch with ¾-inch gravel.

7. Add an inch of organic potting soil.

8. Water the transplants well and space each plant, evenly in the window box.

9. Add soil around the plants and fill the window box with soil, leaving 1 inch of space from the top of the window box.

10. Add a 1-inch layer of mulch on top of the soil and again water thoroughly.

CUISINE GARDEN SIGNS & PLANT MARKERS

Until you can identify all of the plants in your garden by sight, you'll need garden and plant signs—the finishing touch to your garden. You can make these handy signs from scraps of wood; if you'd like a cleaner look, purchase new wood from your local lumberyard or building supply store. For a more rustic look, try using reclaimed wood.

WHAT YOU NEED

- One 5-in. x 18-in. piece of wood of any thickness you like
- Sharpie Permanent Marker (for thinner lines and less bleeding choose ultra-fine point)
- Pencil
- Ruler
- Four 3-in. screws for each sign

Making Garden Signs

1. First, make a drawing or design or write words in pencil on the wood. Use a ruler or a stencil to guide you, if need be.

2. Trace your drawing, design, or words with a marker. To keep the marker from bleeding into the wood, do not apply a lot of pressure.

3. Use the screws to attach the sign to the side of your raised bed.

Making Plant Markers

1. Make a drawing or design or write words in pencil on the wood. If you need it, use a ruler to guide you. Be as creative as you like. If freehand drawing is not your thing, use a stencil.

2. Trace your drawing, design, or words with the marker. To keep the marker from bleeding into the wood, do not apply a lot of pressure.

3. Stick the plant marker in the soil next to the plant in your garden.

WHAT YOU NEED

- 14-in.-long wooden shims
- Sharpie Permanent Marker (for thinner lines and less bleeding choose ultra-fine point)
- Pencil
- Ruler

Part II

CUISINE GARDEN PLANS

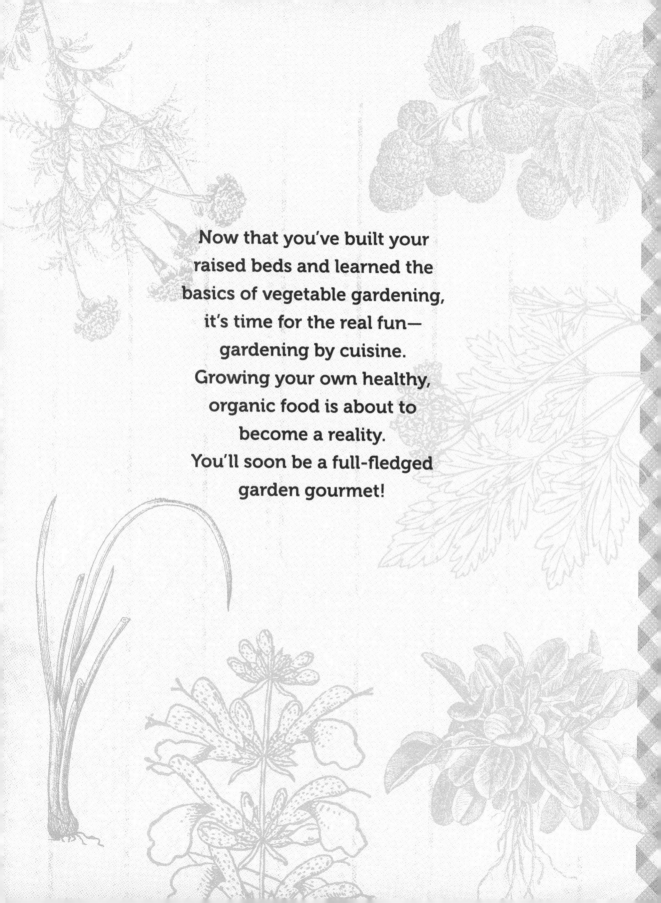

Now that you've built your raised beds and learned the basics of vegetable gardening, it's time for the real fun— gardening by cuisine. Growing your own healthy, organic food is about to become a reality. You'll soon be a full-fledged garden gourmet!

CHAPTER FIVE

HERB PESTO GARDEN

An essential part of cooking delicious food from your garden is the taste of fresh herbs, and lucky for us, they are easy to grow. If you're new to gardening and have no idea where to start, this is the cuisine garden for you.

Herbs are like culinary magic, capable of being processed into lots of different pesto combinations, which you can then add to pasta and use in breads or with meat and fish as flavorings. Although traditionally associated with basil, pesto can be made with many different herbs, so don't be surprised not to find basil in this pesto garden. (See Chapter Thirteen for more on basil and how to grow it.)

The herbs in this bed are great for more than just pesto. One of my favorite uses for fresh herbs is to infuse them in cocktails. These delicious drinks are very refreshing on a warm summer afternoon.

Herbs can be frozen or dried and stored for up to a year, to be used later in myriad ways. Pollinators and other beneficial insects love their flowers, and as companion plants, herbs keep aphids and other bad bugs out of your garden. Herbs are very hardy; once they're established, it's hard to kill them.

THE CULINARY HERB GARDEN

All the culinary herbs in this garden are hardy perennials, so you'll only need to plant them once. You can start a bed for an herb garden from seed at any time of the year, but it's best to start no later than eight weeks before the average first fall frost date in order to give the seeds time to germinate before winter.

Once you start an herb garden, you'll be able to dig up some plants every fall and repot them to grow indoors over the winter or to share with others. At the peak of the growing season and beyond, you will be able to harvest savory tidbits every day and produce pounds of herbs for just pennies.

Herbs are generally tastiest before they flower, but, if you let your plants flower, they'll attract beneficial insects that will pollinate the rest of your veggies' flowers. Also, once you've let your herbs flower and go to seed, you can collect the seeds and plant them next year, or simply do nothing and the plants will self-sow.

The more you harvest off the tops of your plants, the longer it will take them to flower—and the longer you'll be able to enjoy them at the peak of their perfection as ingredients in a variety of fresh and cooked dishes.

In this chapter you'll discover how to grow and preserve several varieties of herbs that will provide you with fresh garden flavors to enjoy not only this year but in the months to come.

What to Plant

In this garden you'll plant Chives, Parsley, Mint, Oregano, Sage, Arugula, Thyme, Sorrel
Difficulty level Easy
Zones All
Sunlight Partial shade to full sun
Earliest planting date Four weeks before the average last spring frost date

Garden Add-ons

Hoop house Protect your plants with a hoop house (see pages 58 and 63) until average nighttime temperatures are in the 50s if you live in zones 3–8 (see the hardiness zones chart on pages 26–27).

USES OF CULINARY HERBS

Herbs can be used, fresh or dried, as seasoning for fish, poultry, beef, or vegetables.

Fresh herbs can be added to salads.

Herb pestos can be made and stored for use as salad dressings and on pastas, grains, or vegetables.

Herbs can be infused in cocktails or added to water as flavorings.

GROWING CULINARY PERENNIAL HERBS

You can start your herb garden from seeds or transplants, beginning four weeks before the average last spring frost date. Sow seeds or transplant herbs according to the garden plan, and cover them with a hoop house until average nighttime temperatures reach 50 degrees.

1. If you are starting your plants from seed, keep the soil moist until the seeds germinate, then allow the soil to dry out between waterings. Once the herb plants are 4 inches high, you should water, weed, and then mulch them.

2. If you're starting your garden from transplants, plant the herbs, mulch them right away, and cover them with a hoop house until average nighttime temperatures reach 50 degrees.

3. If you are starting your herb garden when nighttime temperatures are in the 60s or higher, there's no need to use a hoop house. Keep seeds moist until they germinate, then water plants as deeply as needed, allowing the soil to dry between waterings.

4. When summer temperatures are 90 degrees and above, you will need to water your plants every morning.

Growing Tips

• When summer temperatures are 90 degrees and above, you will need to water every morning and maybe in the evening too.

• Be careful not to wet the leaves of the plants when watering, to prevent diseases. Be careful not to wet the leaves of the herbs when watering them to prevent them from being burned by the sun.

• Few garden pests or diseases affect culinary herbs. Consequently, aromatic herbs are used as companion plants to vegetables in order to deter garden pests. In fact, aromatic herbs are used in many organic insecticidal sprays.

• Harvest herbs regularly by cutting off the tops of the plants. This will keep the plant growing and prevent it from flowering too early. Herbs taste best before they flower.

• Enrich the soil in your garden beds with compost before replanting.

• Use fresh herbs for homemade meals throughout the growing season, or preserve them by drying or freezing them (see page 80).

• As soon as average nighttime temperatures fall into the 50s, put a hoop house on your herb garden to extend the fall harvest.

What is an herb? As used by botanists, the term *herb* refers to an edible plant that dies at the end of the growing season without developing woody tissue; these plants produce seeds and can be annuals, biennials, or perennials.

The word *herb* is also widely used to describe a plant or plant part—flower, leaf, bark, stem, or root—that is valued for its medicinal, savory, or aromatic properties.

Herbs were first used in cooking as a way to keep meat from spoiling and to cover up the strong smell and flavor of the meat when it began to go bad. In the Middle Ages, monks cultivated herb gardens for medicinal uses.
But the lasting impact of herbs on cooking has been for seasoning and flavoring food. It is astonishing how effectively a dish can be transformed from Italian to Asian with the change of a single herb.

PLANTS YOU NEED

Chives
seed
16 per 1 sq. ft.

Parsley
seed
4 per 1 sq. ft.

Mint
seedling
1 per 4 sq. ft.

Oregano
seedling
1 per 4 sq. ft.

Sage
seedling
1 per 4 sq. ft.

Arugula
seed
9 per 1 sq. ft.

Thyme
seed or seedling
1 per 4 sq. ft.

Sorrel
seed
9 per 1 sq. ft.

WINDOW BOX & RAISED-BED GARDEN PLANS

A Window Box Garden

For instructions on building a window box see pages 65–66. To get your garden started, pick four herbs that you will use the most from the options listed under "Plants You Need" and plant them with the appropriate spacing. Choose seedlings in 4-inch pots.

HOW TO GROW HERBS IN A WINDOW BOX

1. Prepare a window box for planting by filling the bottom inch of the box with ¾-inch gravel.

2. Add 1 inch of organic potting soil.

3. Remove the plants from the pots and space them out evenly in the window box.

4. Loosely pack soil around the plants and water thoroughly.

5. Add a layer of mulch to the top of the soil and again thoroughly water the plants.

MAINTENANCE TIPS

• Water container plants daily, as containers can dry out quickly.
• Fertilize once a week with a liquid fertilizer or compost tea (see page 24).
• Add compost, as a mulch, once a month.

Raised-Bed Garden Plans

The herbs I've included in these beds are the go-to herbs for many dishes. Using fresh homegrown herbs makes any meal a treat—and you just can't get the same explosive taste or vibrant color on the plate from store-bought herbs.

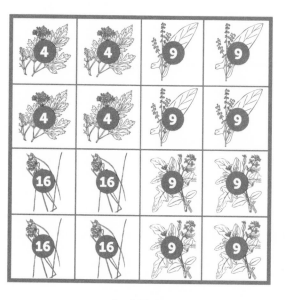

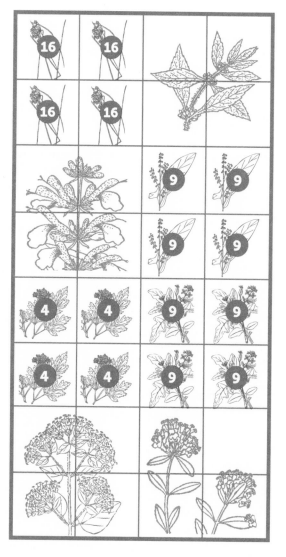

4 x 4 Plans

4 x 8 Plan

CHIVES

Members of the onion family, chives are perennial plants and very easy to grow. You'll use this herb in your cooking more than you may think. Chives are among the hardiest of all herbs.

Seed to table 77–80 days
Spacing for seeds 16 per square foot
Spacing for transplants One 4- to 6-inch pot per square foot
Native to Europe and Asia

Patti's Picks

Garlic Chives (*Allium tuberosum*) This cold-hardy variety has a strong garlic flavor; the edible white flowers are scented and also taste like garlic.
Height 9–12 inches
In bloom Summer

Common Chives (*Allium schoenoprasum*) Used in many dishes, this traditional variety (with purple flowers) is also cold-hardy and has a sweet onion flavor.
Height 12–18 inches
In bloom Spring

PARSLEY

This cool-weather, hardy perennial can last well into winter. Parsley's strong flavor is highlighted when it's finely chopped and used as the finishing touch on pasta dishes and in tabouleh salad.

Seed to table 84–90 days
Spacing for seeds 4 per square foot
Spacing for transplants One 4- to 6-inch pot per square foot
Native to Mediterranean

Patti's Pick

Giant of Italy Parsley (*Petroselinum crispum* var. *neapolitanum*) This is the tastiest, largest, and most prolific of the heirloom parsleys—and it's easy to grow.
Height 18–24 inches
In bloom Summer

MINT

This perennial herb related to oregano, basil, and sage is very fast-growing and adapts to different growing conditions. Mint is an invasive herb that will take over your bed if it is not divided every year.

Seed to table 56–70 days

Spacing for seeds A pinch of seeds in the center of a 4-square-foot plot

Spacing for transplants One 4- to 6-inch container of mint per 4 square feet

Native to Europe and Asia

Patti's Pick

Spearmint (*Mentha spicata*) When a recipe calls for mint, it usually means spearmint. This classic mint variety is perfect for a slew of recipes, from meat marinades to ice cream to tea. It's used in Turkish and Greek cuisines as well as in Indian and Mexican dishes.

Height 12–18 inches

In bloom Summer–fall

OREGANO

A prolific grower, this perennial member of the mint family has a strong flavor and is used in many Italian and Mediterranean recipes. If it is allowed to flower, oregano is a popular herb with bumblebees.

Seed to table 56–70 days

Spacing for seeds A pinch of seeds in the center of a 4-square-foot plot

Spacing for transplants One 4- to 6-inch container per 4 square feet

Native to Mediterranean

Patti's Pick

Oregano (*Origanum vulgare*) This traditional herb flavors many Italian recipes, including tomato marinara. It can also be used medicinally for its antioxidant and anti-microbial properties. Oregano has been used for thousands of years as palliative for stomach and respiratory ailments, and for sore throat, among many other ailments.

Height 18–24 inches

In bloom Summer–fall

SAGE

When dried and powdered, sage is a key ingredient in poultry rubs and stuffing, usually for chicken or turkey, and can be used with other birds as well. A member of the mint family, sage has been used as a culinary herb for more than 5,000 years. It is the highest-yielding herb in your container garden and adds a great touch to a flower bouquet.

Seed to table 80–85 days
Spacing for seeds A pinch of seeds in the center of a 4-square-foot plot
Spacing for transplants One 4- to 6-inch container per 4 square feet
Native to Mediterranean

Patti's Pick

Broadleaf or Common Sage (*Salvia officinalis*) In the spring, the leaves of this plant are a gray-green.
Height. 24–36 inches
In bloom Spring–early summer

ARUGULA

Arugula is easy to grow; if it's allowed to go to seed, it will self-sow and come back year after year. I love making pesto, green salads, and pasta salads with this peppery-tasting herb.

Seed to table. 21–30 days
Spacing for seeds. 9 per square foot
Spacing for transplants One 4- to 6-inch pot per 4 square feet
Native to Mediterranean area, from Morocco and Portugal to Turkey

Patti's Picks

Wild Rocket (aka Roquette; *Eruca vesicaria sativa*) A small, spicy variety used for seasoning.

Sylvetta Arugula (*Rucola selvatica*) A large-leaf, spicy heirloom variety that's perfect for salads.

Apollo Arugula (*Eruca sativa*) A large-leaf, spicy Italian heirloom variety that's also great in salads.
Height 12–18 inches
In bloom Late spring

THYME

A beautiful, tasty herb that grows much like oregano, thyme is a slow-growing perennial, but it's the most essential herb in the garden for seasoning meat and poultry.

Seed to table 90–180 days

Spacing for seeds A pinch of seeds in the center of a 4-square-foot plot

Spacing for transplants One 4- to 6-inch container per 4 square feet

Native to Mediterranean region, and can now be found wherever the winters are mild.

Patti's Pick

English Thyme (*Thymus vulgaris*) A common component for *bouquet garni* and *herbes de Provence*, this traditional variety has been used for millennia. It is often used to flavor lamb, tomatoes, and eggs.

Height 12–18 inches

In bloom Mid-spring

SORREL

The least-known herb in the United States, sorrel is a cool-season perennial that is easy to grow and versatile in the kitchen. Harvest sorrel as soon as the leaves are 2 inches long. **Caution:** Sorrel can be toxic if eaten in large quantities due to the oxalic acid content and should be used sparingly.

Seed to table 70–80 days

Spacing for seeds 9 per square foot

Spacing for transplants One 4- to 6-inch pot per square foot

Native to Europe

Patti's Pick

Garden Sorrel (*Rumex acetosa*) Traditionally, this perennial herb has been used in French and other European cuisines.

Height 18–24 inches

In bloom Late summer–early fall

PRESERVING CULINARY HERBS

To save herbs for later use, you can dry or even freeze them

HOW TO DRY HERBS: OREGANO, SAGE

1. Harvest fresh herbs in the late afternoon and place them in bunches in brown paper bags.

2. Store the bags in a cool dark place.

3. Check the herbs after two weeks and remove any moldy herbs.

4. Put the herbs back in the bag and store them in a dark place for two more weeks or until they are dry. You can also use a dehydrator (an appliance that removes moisture from food in order to preserve it) to dry herbs overnight.

5. With the leaves on the stem, store herbs in airtight glass jars.

6. When you're ready to use them, pick leaves off the stems and crush the leaves as needed to release the flavors and aromas.

HOW TO FREEZE FRESH HERBS:
CHIVES, ARUGULA, PARSLEY, MINT, & SORREL

1. After harvesting the herbs, pick the leaves off the stems.

2. Place fresh herb leaves in ice-cube trays—as many as you can fit—then cover the herbs with hot water and put the trays in the freezer.

3. You can also make an herb paste using a food processor. Then put the paste in the ice-cube trays, two-thirds of the way full, and freeze.

4. Once the ice cubes are frozen, put them into freezer-safe Ziploc bags. Then label and put the cubes back into the freezer; they will keep for up to a year.

5. When you want to cook with the herbs, there's no need to defrost them. Simply pop the frozen herb cube right into the pot.

6. For day-to-day use, cover dried herbs with 1 inch of water in a jar. Tighten the lid and store the jar in the fridge.

RECIPES FOR HERB MIXES

Seasoning & Marinades

Mix equal parts of minced **oregano, parsley**, and **sage** (fresh or dried). Use these herbs fresh in salad dressings and meat marinades. This mix is delicious sprinkled on hot garlic bread.

For seasoning beef, combine equal parts of **minced parsley, thyme,** and **oregano** with **minced onion, crushed garlic,** and enough **olive oil** to make a paste, and place the ingredients in a mixer. Add **red wine vinegar** and **pepper**, and mix. Allow the beef to sit in the marinade for at least four hours.

To marinate chicken, use equal parts of **parsley, sage,** and **thyme,** with olive oil and garlic.

Mint Pesto Marinade

Makes 2½ cups

This pesto adds a Mediterranean twist, especially to lamb and beef.

1	cup packed mint leaves
½	cup flat-leaf parsley leaves
½	cup minced chives
2	medium garlic cloves
½	teaspoon finely grated lemon zest
	Juice of half a lemon or lime
4	tablespoons extra-virgin olive oil
	Salt and pepper to taste

In a food processor, combine the first six ingredients and pulse until chopped. With the processor on low, add the olive oil in a slow stream and pulse until the pesto is paste- like. Season with salt and pepper to taste. Mix. Toss the pesto with goat cheese and pasta to make a hearty salad, or use it as a seasoning for lamb or grilled burgers.

Six-Herb Pesto

Makes 5 cups

With this recipe you can use almost every herb in your garden for a fresh, flavorful pesto. With every bite you'll taste a variety of different herbs. Make an extra batch and freeze it for a summer-fresh dish next winter.

1	cup fresh arugula leaves
1	cup fresh parsley leaves
½	cup fresh mint leaves
¼	cup fresh oregano leaves
¼	cup fresh sage leaves
½	cup finely chopped fresh chives
½	cup coarsely chopped pine nuts
	Juice of half a lemon
¼	cup grated Parmesan cheese, more to taste
2	cloves garlic (or more, if desired), sliced
½	cup olive oil or more

Put the ingredients into a food processor and pulse while adding olive oil until the mixture has a paste-like consistency. This herb pesto can be made ahead of time and refrigerated for up to two weeks or frozen for up to six months. It is delicious as a salad dressing, a dip for vegetables, or a sandwich spread. To serve Six-Herb Pesto with pasta, use 3 cups of pesto per pound of pasta and stir in a half cup of boiling pasta water.

Simple Fresh-Herb Pesto

Yield varies

Use any of the culinary herbs from your garden for this recipe.

Mince garlic and add equal parts **fresh herbs, pignoli nuts,** and **grated Parmesan cheese.** Chop in mixer and pulse in **olive oil** until the mixture is a loose paste, then add freshly ground **salt and pepper** to taste.

Sorrel Pesto

Makes 3 cups

This pesto works beautifully in cold pasta salads and as a marinade for fish.

2	cups sorrel
½	cup parsley
4	cloves organic garlic
1	cup freshly grated Parmesan cheese
½	cup pine nuts or walnuts
½	cup olive oil
	Salt and pepper to taste

Mix the ingredients in a blender until smooth.

Variation. For pasta seasoning, add ½ cup pasta water to 3 cups sorrel pesto for every pound of pasta and mix together in a bowl while the pasta is hot.

Tabouleh Salad

Finely chop and mix equal parts of **parsley, garlic chives**, and **mint**. Add finely chopped **tomato, cucumber,** and **green onion; cracked bulgur wheat** (prepared according to package instructions); and **lemon juice, olive oil, salt,** and **pepper** to taste. This Middle Eastern salad is served, on the side, with falafel, hummus, and pita bread.

Herb Butter for Broiled Fish

Mix together 1 stick of softened unsalted organic **butter**, ¼ cup finely chopped **parsley**, and ¼ cup finely minced **chives**. Store the mixture in the freezer or refrigerator. Use half the herb butter as a marinade on a pound of your choice of fish (haddock works well), or slather the fish with the mixture after it comes out of the broiler. Save a little herb butter to serve on the side.

Mini Pizzas with Goat Cheese, Herb Pesto, & Fresh Arugula

Makes 6 mini pizzas

This healthy pizza recipe is perfect for an appetizer — and a great way to introduce kids to different herb flavors. When you serve up these mini pizzas you'll feel like a garden gourmet!

For the Pizza Dough

3½	cups self-rising flour
1	cup of wheat flour
1½	cups hot water
½	cup vegetable oil

Mix all ingredients and work into a dough. Dust a counter with flour. Divide the dough into six equal pieces. Store the dough in the fridge wrapped in cellophane until you are ready to make the pizzas.

For the Mini Pizzas

2	cups fresh arugula
8	oz. goat cheese
1	cup herb pesto

Preheat oven to 450°F

Dust a counter with flour. Using a rolling pin, roll out each piece of dough thinly (no thicker than ¼ inch). Place the dough on a pizza baking pan and bake in oven for 5 minutes to partially cook. Remove the pizzas from oven and add 1 tablespoon of herb pesto to the center of each one, spreading out the pesto evenly. Add goat cheese. Put the pizzas back in the oven and bake for 5 minutes or until crusts are brown. Remove the pizzas from the oven and sprinkle with fresh baby arugula. Serve immediately.

Garden Mojito

Makes 1 cocktail

The mojito—a popular Cuban drink that has recently made it up north—is a great summer cocktail to make any evening before dinner.

10	fresh spearmint leaves and a sprig of mint for garnish
¼	cup simple syrup made with organic cane sugar
2	oz. seltzer water
2	oz. white Bacardi rum
	Juice of one lime
	Crushed ice

In a cocktail shaker, combine 10 mint leaves with sugar-cane syrup and muddle with a wooden spoon. Add seltzer, rum, lime juice, ice, and shake for 15 to 30 seconds.

In a chilled tumbler, add a sprig of mint and fill with ice. Pour in contents of shaker, enjoy, and make more. When it's in season, add a strip of sugar cane to the mojito, and suck on it after you've finished the drink. Delicious.

Organic Herb-Infused Ice Water

Makes 2 cups

Kick the bottled water habit by making your own organic, herb-infused ice water. You'll reduce plastic waste, save money, and be healthier. This is a zero-calorie drink.

Brew 2 ounces of your favorite herbs in 2 cups of hot water for two minutes. Strain the herbs, and let the water cool for at least ten minutes. Store the herb-infused water in the fridge in a pitcher or pour it right into a reusable water bottle.

CHAPTER SIX

ASIAN STIR-FRY & SALAD GARDEN

The greens in this cuisine garden come straight from the gardens and woks of Southeast Asia, and the recipes are inspired by one of my favorite salads from the area—Thai Cabbage Salad. It makes all my taste buds tingle, and my desire for a crunchy dinner is more than satisfied by this simple, carbohydrate-free dish.

Not only will you be able to grow all the ingredients for Thai Cabbage Salad in your own garden—you can also use the same ingredients to make great stir-fries. Just add meat, poultry, or seafood to the basic recipe (see page 105) and you can make a different Asian meal every day of the week. Because salad greens grow very quickly, you can begin harvesting a mixture of Asian greens, including the mighty bok choy, in about a month. The first crop can be planted in a raised bed from seed as early as five weeks before the average last (spring) frost date (see "Determining Frost Dates" on page 25). The minimum amount you'd spend on purchasing seedlings—or the $18 or so you'd shell out for six seed packets—is far less than you'd spend on a single meal at a Thai restaurant on date night.

And if you have no experience with making Asian food, think of this garden and the recipes in this chapter as an opportunity to expand your culinary skills. Don't worry. No matter what you do, you can't make a bad meal when you start with ingredients fresh from the garden.
Get your chopsticks ready, everybody!

THE ASIAN GARDEN

I'm cramming a lot into this garden, but you'll see that a little goes along way. Many of the traditional Asian plants you'll be growing are perennials in subtropical and tropical climates, so if you live in zones 9–10 you can keep them growing outside all year long; if you live in zone 8 you can protect them in a hoop house when there's a cold snap. For the rest of us they are a seasonal pleasure. After you've gotten the hang of growing an Asian garden and started to enjoy the fresh tastes of this cuisine, you'll never look at takeout the same way again, I promise.

What to Plant

In this garden you'll plant Asian greens, Bunching onions, Snow peas, Cucumbers, Hot peppers, Asian eggplants, Culinary herbs (Cilantro, Basil, Lemongrass)
Difficulty level Easy
Zones All
Sunlight Full sun
Earliest planting date Five weeks before the average last spring frost

Garden Add-ons

Hoop house If you live in zones 3–8, protect your garden with a hoop house (see pages 58 and 63) until average nighttime temps are in the 50s.
Trellis You can grow cucumbers vertically to maximize your growing space and produce super-straight cucumbers.

PLANTS YOU NEED

Asian Greens
seed
16 per 1 sq. ft.

Bunching Onions
seed
16 per 1 sq. ft.

Snow Peas
seed or seedling
9 per 1 sq. ft.

Cucumbers
seed or seedling
2 per 1 sq. ft.

Asian Eggplant
seedling
1 per 2 sq. ft.

Hot Peppers
seedling
1 per 2 sq. ft.

Basil
seed
4 per 1 sq. ft.

Lemongrass
seedling
1 per 4 sq. ft.

Cilantro
seed
9 per 1 sq. ft.

CONTAINER & RAISED-BED GARDEN PLANS

- One 18-gal. galvanized container
- Gravel or filler for proper drainage, enough for a 2-in. layer at the bottom of the container
- Organic potting soil, about 2 cu. ft.
- Seeds and plants

Container Garden Plan: 18-Gallon Container

You don't need to spend a fortune on a large container. A galvanized 18-gallon tub costing less than $20 will do, and you'll be able to harvest from it weekly.

PREPARING THE CONTAINER

1. Make at least 20 drainage holes in the bottom of the container using a large (¼-inch) nail and a hammer.

2. Fill the bottom of the container with a 2-inch layer of ¾-inch gravel or a lighter substitute.

3. Add organic potting soil up to 2 inches from the top of the container and water thoroughly.

WHEN TO PLANT

1. Sow seeds according to the diagram starting five weeks before the average last spring frost date, and cover with a mini hoop house until nighttime temperatures are in the 60s.

2. Plant eggplant or hot peppers starting four weeks after the average last spring frost date.

MAINTENANCE TIPS

- Containers dry out quickly and need to be watered almost daily.
- Once a week, fertilize the soil in the container with liquid fertilizer or compost tea.
- Once a month, add a thin layer of compost (as mulch).

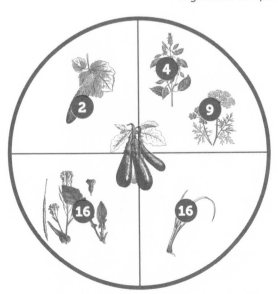

Container Plan

Raised-Bed Garden Plans

This is one of my favorite raised beds because it's really easy to plant and keep going. In fact, the greens and snow peas you start in the early spring can be replanted in late summer for a fall harvest. You'll be eating Asian veggies in no time!

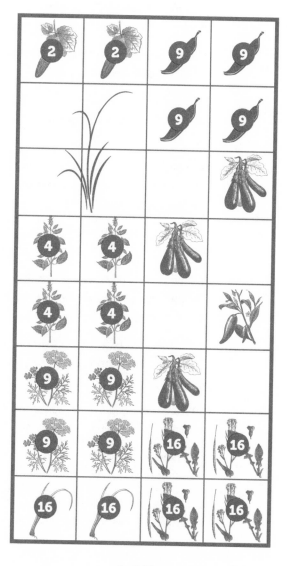

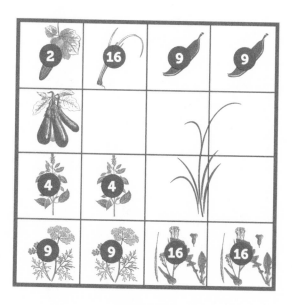

4 x 4 Plan

4 x 8 Plan

GROWING ASIAN PLANTS & HERBS

1. Start your Asian garden from seed.

2. First, water your garden soil thoroughly and put your planting grid in place.

3. Five weeks before the average last spring frost date, sow Asian greens, snow peas, and bunching onions according to the instructions given in the sections that follow. Tracing with your finger, divide each square foot into the appropriate number of smaller squares.

4. Sow a pinch of seeds in the center of each new square. Press seeds gently into the soil and cover lightly.

5. Cover with a hoop house until average nighttime temperatures reach 50 degrees. Keep the soil moist until the seeds germinate, then allow the soil to dry out between waterings.

6. In about one week your peas and greens will sprout first, and you'll be able to eat baby greens and pea shoots about four weeks after planting (depending on climate conditions).

7. One week after the average last spring frost date, sow cucumber, cilantro, and basil seeds, and plant eggplant, pepper, and lemongrass seedlings.

8. If you've already eaten the greens or anything else in the garden, now will be a good time to replant them. Keep sowing greens throughout the growing season.

9. Keep the hoop house on your plants until nighttime temperatures average in the 60s; then remove it. Once you remove the hoop house, attach the trellis to the end of the bed where the cucumbers and snow peas are growing.

10. Weed the garden, and add a 1-inch layer of mulch. Water regularly, allowing the garden to dry between waterings.

11. Harvest greens, herbs, and veggies often, and replant at any time throughout the growing season for additional harvests.

12. Two weeks before the average first fall frost date, put the hoop house back over the garden to extend your harvest into the winter.

ASIAN GREENS

Asian greens are simply a mix of Asian mustards such as early mazuna (also known as mizuna) and a variety of braising greens such as bok choy, as well as michili cabbage. You can buy a packet of seeds that contains a variety of Asian greens, or you can make your own mixture, using seeds from your favorite greens. The seeds will stay viable for at least three or four sowings, depending on the climate.

Seed to table 21 days

Spacing for seeds 16 per square foot

Spacing for transplants One 4- to 6-inch pot per square foot

Native to Asia

HEALTH BENEFITS

The nutrients in Asian greens help prevent certain cancers and relieve stress. In addition, these nutrient-dense super-foods contain loads of vitamins A and E, along with minerals such as zinc and magnesium. And they're a great source of calcium.

Patti's Pick

Siamese Dragon Mix This is a variety of Asian greens that are mixed and grown together. Baby Asian greens should be eaten fresh when the leaves are between 2 and 4 inches long.

Height: 8–24 inches

PESTS & DISEASES

Slugs and snails, as well as aphids, beetles, and caterpillars, will feast on your greens unless you check your garden regularly and get rid of them right away. Diseases such as leaf spot and mildew can affect your greens too, but if you harvest your crops often, diseases won't have a chance to affect them.

HARVESTING GREENS

You'll be able to harvest nutrient-rich Asian greens as early as three weeks after planting, when the leaves are at least 2 inches tall for salads and at least 4 inches tall for stir-fries. Take a bowl and a pair of scissors out to the garden; clip the largest leaves at the soil line and place them in the bowl. Leave the rest of the plant in the garden so it can continue to grow.

BUNCHING ONIONS

Bunching onions (also known as scallions or green onions) grow in bunches and do not form a bulb, so they don't need as much room in your garden as larger onion varieties do. Bunching onions are ready for harvest early in the growing season, when their long, green-and-white spears are about the length and width of a number-2 pencil. This is a perfect time to make Scallion Pancakes with Ginger & Lemongrass Dipping Sauce (see page 103 for the recipe), a family favorite. Growing these types of onions will become a personal mission when you see how easy they are to grow and how great they are on the plate.

Seed to table 60 days

Spacing for seeds 16 per square foot

Spacing for transplants Start these from seed. Bunching onions are not readily found as transplants.

Native to Asia

Patti's Pick

Tokyo Long White (*Allium fistulosum*) These green onions are the real deal. You'll be harvesting and adding them to many meals, even if they're not Asian dishes.

Height 18–24 inches

PESTS & DISEASES

Some pests, such as aphids, and some diseases, such as wilt and rot, can strike your bunching onions, but these onions are a quick-growing crop, and if you harvest them regularly, you shouldn't have a problem with pests or diseases.

HARVESTING BUNCHING ONIONS

Pull out as many onions as you need, roots and all. Once you've eaten half of your harvest, sow more seeds. Keep sowing into the fall. These onions are cold-hardy evergreen plants, so they will last well into the winter, with protection, and bounce back in early spring, even if there's snow on the ground.

SNOW PEAS

Snow peas are easy to grow; they're high in vitamin C and dietary fiber and can be prepared in a variety of ways. Try the recipe for Mixed Asian Greens & Pea Shoots with Soy-Ginger Vinaigrette (page 101) and see how easy it is to become a convert to tender, sweet pea shoots. You can start planting these cold-hardy veggies five weeks before the last frost date.

Seed to table shoots: 30 days; pods: 60 days
Spacing for seeds 9 per square foot
Spacing for transplants 9 per square foot
Native to Asia

Patti's Pick

Oregon Sugar Pod (_Pisum sativum_) These are a crispy, cool, and delicious raw snack.
Height of vines 24–36 inches

PESTS & DISEASES

Don't be horrified if you see little holes in the leaves of your snow pea plants—you're doing things right and practicing organic gardening. Common garden pests may move in, but your plants will be fine if you stay vigilant and remove any pests and brown, dead, or diseased leaves.

HARVESTING SNOW PEAS

Before snow peas start to flower, when the plants are about 8 inches tall, you can harvest pea shoots—about 4 inches from the top of the plants—and add them to a salad or stir-fry. Anytime I'm outside tending to the garden, I pop off a few pea shoots for a delicious snack. In no time, these peas start growing little white flowers, which are also edible. Just don't pick too many of them because that's where the snow-pea pod forms. Harvest snow peas when the pods are thin and young. They're delicious eaten raw in salads. Slightly larger pods are great for stir-frying. Try them at every stage of growth to discover the way you like them most.

ASIAN EGGPLANTS

I love growing Asian eggplants. They're hard to find in the super-market, and they taste so good when they're freshly picked and added to the evening meal. In fact, this is the only type of eggplant my husband will eat, and that's a huge endorsement.

Asian eggplants are compact plants, so they grow well in raised beds and small spaces. If you can't find plants for Asian eggplant at your garden center, feel free to substitute other varieties. Asian egg-plants are unique-looking, too. They can be small and round or thin and long, and they come in an amazing array of colors.

Eggplants can be started from seed right in the raised bed in cli-mates starting in zone 9 (or warmer). Plant 2 seeds per square foot. Thin out the seedlings by removing all but the strongest, healthiest, and largest seedlings, leaving about 24 inches between plants. In warm climates, you can keep the plants growing for several years, as long as you care for them and Mother Nature cooperates. In zones 8 (or cooler), dig up some of your eggplants in the fall, plant them in a container, bring them indoors, and see how long you can grow them.

From seed to table 70–80 days

Spacing for transplants 1 plant per 2 square feet

Native to India

Patti's Picks

Ping Tung (*Solanum melongena* var. *esculentum*) These easy-to-grow, sweet, and tender eggplants are great for grilling and add an exotic twist.

Ichiban Japanese Eggplant (*Solanum melongena* var. *ichiban*) This long, purple variety is easy to grow and is prolific, especially in warmer climates with long growing sesons. Ichiban is a good choice for cooler climates as well.

Thai Green Eggplant (*Solanum melongena* var. *esculentum*) This is the same eggplant type as ping tung, but the fruit is green, rather than purple, and it has a milder flavor when eaten raw, but it is just as delicious as ping tung when you cook it.

Height 24–32 inches

PESTS & DISEASES

Eggplants suffer from the same diseases as other plants in the night-shade family, such as tomatoes, so beware of the common garden pests and diseases that afflict them.

HARVESTING ASIAN EGGPLANTS

Harvest young eggplants when they are about 6 inches long. They're delicious! Your plants will generate more fruit every time you harvest, so don't let your eggplants stay on the vine until they rot.

HOT PEPPERS

Hot peppers grow best in super-hot climates, like New Mexico's, where there's little rain, but you can grow great hot peppers almost anywhere. They can be hard to start from seed, however. When you buy a hot pepper plant from your garden center, make sure a few peppers—or at least multiple flowers—are growing on it.

Seed to table 90 days
Spacing for transplants 1 per 2 square feet
Native to Southeast Asia

Patti's Pick

Thai Hot Chili Pepper (*Capsicum frutescens*) This is the traditional hot pepper of Thai cuisine. The thin peppers on this tropical plant stick straight up in the air; they start off green, then turn red when they're ripe and blazing hot.

Height Up to 2 feet

PESTS & DISEASES

Beware of all common vegetable garden pests and diseases. Refer to pages Chapter Two to learn more about protecting your plants.

HARVESTING HOT PEPPERS

When these peppers are green they are plenty hot, so feel free to prune as many as you need with a pair of scissors. Allow some to turn red for the strongest heat to emerge. Make sure to wash your hands after handling these peppers, and be especially careful not to rub your eyes. Ouch! Keep hot peppers away from kids.

CUCUMBERS

Cucumbers are great in Asian dishes. Their crunch and flavor in my Thai Cucumber Salad recipe (see page 102) is a delight. Cucumbers are very low in calories and high in nutrients and water. You're going organic, so don't worry—it's safe to eat the skin, which is also high in dietary fiber. Because cucumbers grow on vines, you can plant them vertically. Just help them grow upward by providing a trellis, and the tendrils will do the rest.

Seed to table 55–60 days
Spacing for seeds and transplants 2 per square foot
Native to Mediterranean and south Asia

Patti's Picks

Thai Green Cucumber (*Cucumis sativus*) This 6- to 8-inch pickling cucumber is great eaten young and fresh in salads.

Suyo Long Cucumber (*Cucumis sativus*) This is a funky, bumpy Japanese cucumber. When trained on a trellis, suyo longs grow super straight and long (18 inches or longer), and can feed a lot of people. I love picking and eating them when they are babies, when they're about 12 inches long, but I always let a few cucumbers grow as long as they want to grow before I harvest them.

Height 6+ feet

PESTS & DISEASES

Common pests and diseases, such as cucumber beetle or powdery mildew, can affect cucumbers. (Refer to pages 34–39 for more information about pests and diseases.) Treat your plants accordingly as soon as you notice pests, and be vigilant in removing any dead or yellowed leaves.

HARVESTING CUCUMBERS

Using a pair of kitchen scissors, clip off the cucumber at the stem. Under cold running water, remove any small spikes on the cucumber before preparing it. To save cucumber seeds, let a couple cucumbers grow until they're overripe. Scoop out the seeds and rinse off any remaining cucumber flesh. Place the seeds on a paper plate and let them dry in a cool dark place. Store the seeds in a paper bag or Ziploc baggie until spring.

BASIL

For more information about basil, see page 215.
Seed to table 75–80 days
Spacing for seeds 4 per square foot
Spacing for transplants One 4- to 6-inch pot per square foot
Native to India and Southern Asia

Patti's Pick

Thai Basil (*Ocimum basilicum*) This basil is grown the same way as many other types of basils, but its distinctive licorice flavor, particularly in rice stir-fries, makes the taste uniquely Asian. Thai basil leaves are small and narrow, with purple-hued stems and an edible pink-purple bloom.
Height 24–32 inches
In bloom Summer

PESTS & DISEASES

No known pests or diseases affect these aromatic culinary herbs. In fact, they actually help keep garden pests away.

HARVESTING THAI BASIL

Before the herb flowers, clip off the top leaves anytime you want to use them in the kitchen—the herb will continue to grow.

SAVING THE SEEDS

The blooms on Thai basil plants are so pretty (as well as so good to eat) that I can't resist letting some of them flower. Once the flower heads have seeds, allow them to dry before clipping them. Separate the seeds and store them in a plastic baggie or paper bag in a cool, dark place until spring, or use them to start a few indoor herb containers for the winter.

LEMONGRASS

This tropical plant grows rather vigorously in the garden and needs lots of room to grow. You'll need to start your lemongrass plants from a potted plant, purchased from a nursery, or you can start your own by purchasing intact lemongrass stalks from an Asian specialty market. Just place the stalks in about 2 inches of water in a jar until the roots are at least 2 inches long; this should take about two weeks. Then plant the lemongrass in the garden and water it thoroughly. Lemongrass also grows well in containers. Make sure to keep it well watered.

Once the plants are established, you'll be able to harvest lemongrass regularly. I find that I consistently harvest lemongrass for teas (hot and iced), as well as soups, sauces, salads, and stir-fries. You'll want to use this herb even in the winter for its medicinal properties, which help relieve cold symptoms. Just dig it out of your raised bed in the fall, replant it in a pot, and continue to grow lemongrass inside.

Spacing for transplants One 4- to 6-inch pot per 4 square foot
Native to Southeast Asia

Patti's Pick

Lemongrass (*Cymbopogon citrates*). This variety of lemongrass is commonly found in the United States, and you can start your outdoor plants from a cutting, purchased locally, or from seed in order to start growing plants indoors in the winter. In tropical climates you can plant this variety once and it will continue to grow for several years.

Height 4–6 feet; width: 3 feet
In bloom Fall

HARVESTING LEMONGRASS

The best time to harvest lemongrass is right before you want to use it. To harvest lemongrass, dig around the base of the plant and snap or cut off an entire stalk, each of which consists of multiple blades of grass. Let the plant continue to grow so that you can harvest more stalks of lemongrass every 3 or 4 months. Use the bottom part of the stalk in recipes that call for lemongrass and the entire stalk for brewing tea (one stalk for every cup you want to make).

CILANTRO

Cilantro, also known as coriander, is a warm-season culinary herb that is essential to Asian cuisine, among many others. Not only are the leaves used for their intense, unmistakable flavor, but the seeds spice things up too. Try cilantro in my recipe for refreshing Thai Cucumber Salad on page 102. You'll also find that cilantro is really easy to start from seed.

Here's an interesting fact: I've met a few people who will not eat anything made with cilantro—something I could never understand until I learned that some people are genetically predisposed to not like cilantro and are repulsed by the taste.

Seed to table 55 days
Spacing for seeds 9 per square foot
Spacing for transplants One 4- to 6-inch pot per square foot
Native to Mediterranean and Southern Asia

Patti's Pick

Cilantro (*Coriandrum sativum*). The strong-flavored leaves of this classic cilantro are used in Asian, Mexican, and Middle Eastern cuisine. Save the seeds for next year, or use them as a spice in the kitchen.
Height 18–24 inches

RECIPES FOR AN ASIAN STIR-FRY & SALAD GARDEN

I've put my own garden-fresh twists on some traditional Asian recipes in this chapter. You'll need a few simple kitchen tools and ingredients before you get started on these light and healthy treats. For stir-fries, you'll want to use a wok; for steaming rice, a bamboo steamer will do the job. You'll also want to stock up on low-sodium soy sauce, mirin (a kind of rice wine), sesame-seed oil, grape-seed oil, and a stash of fresh ginger root. Let's get started.

Thai Eggplant with Chili Pepper & Thai Basil

Serves four

If you like spicy food, you will love this dish—and it's a great way to show off both your gardening skills and your culinary chops.

1	tbsp. sesame oil
2	Thai hot peppers
3	cloves garlic, minced
3	Thai eggplants (a mix of green and purple eggplants), skin on, sliced into 2-in. irregular pieces
1	cup water
2	tbsp. fish sauce (substitute low-sodium soy sauce for vegetarian option)
1	tbsp. sugar
1	cup Thai basil leaves
3	cups thinly sliced Asian greens

Heat a wok on high and add sesame oil, seeded and sliced hot peppers, and minced garlic. Stir. Add eggplant pieces and stir. Add water, stir, cover tightly, and cook eggplant for about 5 minutes on medium heat. When water has evaporated, stir in fish sauce and sugar. Turn off heat. Toss Thai basil leaves and Asian greens with the eggplant. Serve with brown rice while hot.

Mixed Asian Greens & Pea Shoots with Soy-Ginger Vinaigrette

Serves four

This is another recipe that delivers big flavors with very little effort or equipment. All you need is a large bowl for the greens and a jar in which to make and store the vinaigrette.

For the Soy-Ginger Vinaigrette

½	cup grape-seed oil
2	tbsp. sesame oil
3	tbsp. mirin
2	tbsp. low-sodium soy sauce
1	tsp. grated fresh ginger
3–5	bunching onions, finely chopped
1	tbsp. finely chopped cilantro

Mix ingredients in a jar, cover, and store in the fridge until you need the vinaigrette.

For the Salad

3	cups mixed Asian greens
2	cups fresh pea shoots
	Soy-Ginger Vinaigrette

Combine greens and pea shoots in a large bowl. Right before serving, toss with the vinaigrette, one tablespoon at a time, to coat the greens to taste. Plate immediately and serve.

FISH SAUCE (NAM PLA)

One of the basic ingredients of Thai cooking, fish sauce is used as a condiment as well as a marinade for meat and fish.

Fish sauce is made from a mixture of fermented raw fish and sea salt.

It can be purchased at most supermarkets and specialty grocery stores. Vegetarians can substitute low-sodium soy sauce for fish sauce in most recipes.

Thai Cucumber Salad

Serves four

This is an excellent salad to share at summer barbecues. Make plenty of the dressing and store it in the fridge. Just slice up the cukes for a quick salad to go along with dinner.

For the Dressing

1	Thai hot pepper, seeded and minced
	Juice of 1 lime
4	cloves garlic, minced
3	tbsp. soy sauce
4	tbsp. fish sauce
2	tsp. organic sugar
1	tbsp. lemongrass, minced

For the Salad

2	young Thai green cucumbers or 1 young suyo long cucumber (make sure seeds are not fully formed)
2	green onions, thinly sliced
1	cup coarsely chopped cilantro leaves

Make the dressing by combining all the ingredients in a bowl with a whisk or small fork; then place in the fridge. Using a mandolin or kitchen knife, cut a cucumber into thin strips (don't peel it). Put the strips in a bowl, add the onions and cilantro, and mix. Store in fridge until you're ready to serve. Before serving, toss half the dressing with the cucumber. Add more to taste.

Scallion Pancakes with Ginger & Lemongrass Dipping Sauce

Serves four (but I've been known to eat a whole batch myself)

This delicious, light, crunchy side dish is messy, but once you've tried it, you'll never again want to order it at a restaurant.

For the Ginger & Lemongrass Dipping Sauce

1	tbsp. grated fresh ginger
1	scallion stalk, finely chopped
1	lemongrass stalk, thinly sliced
1	tbsp. low-sodium soy sauce
2	tbsp. sesame oil
1	tbsp. rice wine vinegar
1	tbsp. sugar
1	small red chili, seeded and minced
1	tsp. sesame seeds

Place ingredients in a jar, cover, and shake (to mix).

For the Pancakes

2	cups white flour
2	cups water
1	cup coarsely chopped bunching onions (scallions), marinated in grape-seed oil
1	cup grape-seed oil

Make the dough by mixing the flour and water in a bowl. Cover bowl with a clean dishcloth and let it sit on a counter for 30 minutes. Work the dough on a floured surface and break it up into 4–6 equal pieces. Clean the surface, then drizzle grape-seed oil on it. Roll out each piece of dough into a thin pancake and sprinkle with marinated scallions. Roll each pancake into a snake and shape it like a snail's shell. Wrap each of the snail-shaped pieces in plastic wrap and let them sit on the kitchen counter for another half hour. Remove each piece and roll it out on an oiled surface until it's about 6 inches in diameter. Fry the pancakes in a pan with grape-seed oil until both sides are golden brown. Serve immediately with Ginger & Lemongrass Dipping Sauce.

Cucumber & Eggplant Kimchi

Makes 10 or more generous servings

I can't help sharing this healthy Korean dish with you. Preparation methods vary from region to region in Korea, but this recipe will make you a fan. Kimchi is the most popular food eaten in Korea, where an average of 40 pounds per person is consumed every winter. And it's a great way to extend and preserve your harvest.

Typically kimchi is prepared with fermented Asian cabbage, but you can make it with cucumbers or eggplants, too. Kimchi is so good for you, particularly for your digestion, because of all the good bacteria that are produced during the fermentation process; they help promote the growth of healthy flora in the intestines, much as yogurt and other probiotics do. You can serve kimchi as a side dish or use it as filling in a rice-paper wrap for a unique and healthy spring roll.

3	Thai cucumbers or 1 suyo long cucumber
3	Thai green eggplants or 3 Ichiban eggplants, sliced
2	cups cabbage (optional)
2	tbsp. salt
2	tbsp. minced garlic
1	cup coarsely chopped bunching onions
1	cup garlic chives, coarsely chopped into 2-in. pieces (optional)
2	tbsp. honey or sugar
½	cup Korean red chili powder

Slice the cucumbers and eggplants, leaving the skin on (remember, it's healthy for you). In a large bowl, add the cabbage (if using) to the cucumber and eggplant slices. Sprinkle with salt and toss. Cover the bowl and let it sit for 1 hour. Add the garlic, bunching onions, garlic chives, honey or sugar, and chili powder. Wearing kitchen gloves, toss the veggies to coat them well. Spoon the mixture into a glass jar and cover. (Set some aside for immediate consumption, if you like.) Store in a cool, dark place for one or two days to let the kimchi ferment. When you see froth-like bubbles on top of the mixture, the fermentation process has taken place. Pop the kimchi into the fridge for up to three weeks and eat up!

Thai Cabbage Salad

Serves four

This refreshing recipe puts a spicy Asian twist on your average salad. The flavor is fantastic, and the rolled up cabbage leaves give it a fun and hearty texture.

For the Thai Vinaigrette

1	tbsp. lime juice
1	tbsp. rice wine vinegar
1	tbsp. sesame oil
1	tbsp. mirin
1	tbsp. fish sauce
1	Thai hot pepper
	Salt (to taste)
1	tsp. sugar

Mix lime juice, rice wine vinegar, sesame oil, mirin, fish sauce, Thai hot pepper, salt, and sugar into a small bowl. Stir, then set aside.

For the Thai Cabbage Salad

1	Chinese cabbage (4–6 leaves)
	Mixed Asian greens
	Cilantro (to taste)
	Sliced dark-purple opal basil (to taste)
¼	cup shredded carrots
1	thickly sliced red bell pepper
¼	cup thickly sliced red onions
1	sprig chopped mint

Cut the stems from the Chinese cabbage leaves. Stack three cabbage leaves, then roll up the leaves, starting at the rounded edge. Slice the rolled leaves into ⅛-inch to ¼-inch sections. Place in salad bowl, and mix in other chopped greens and vegetables. Add vinaigrette, toss, and it's ready to serve. If desired, add crushed peanuts for extra flavor.

Asian Stir-Fry

Serves two

Stir-fry is a quick and easy way to get all of your food groups on one plate. Plus, there's a lot of room for creativity, so try some new marinades or different meats to change things up.

	Asian BBQ marinade (available at supermarkets and specialty food shops)
2	lbs. beef, cut into 1- to 2-in. cubes
5	cloves organic garlic (or to taste), peeled
2–3	shallots, peeled
1	tbsp. sesame seed oil
	Mixed Asian greens

Choose a spicy Asian marinade and let the beef cubes sit in it overnight. Place a wok on the stove over medium to high heat. Coarsely chop garlic and shallots. When ready, add a splash of oil to the wok, then add shallots and garlic. Stir until the garlic begins to brown, then add the marinated beef. While the beef is cooking, chop Asian greens to a normal size for salads. Stir the beef occasionally; once it is cooked to your liking, add the Asian greens. Place them on top, then fold them in with the rest of ingredients. After the greens have had a minute to cook, remove from the wok, and serve alone or over rice if desired.

Cucumber & Lemongrass Ice Water

Makes 4–6 cups

All you need for this simple and refreshing beverage is a glass pitcher, a long wooden spoon, and a pot for boiling water.

1   cup coarsely chopped lemongrass

1   cucumber

    Water

    Ice

Wash and slice the cucumber into ¼-inch rounds. Place the chopped lemongrass in a pot of water and allow it to boil for 2 minutes. Remove from heat and cool. Place ice and fresh cucumber slices in a pitcher, then add lemongrass and water, and stir with a wooden spoon. To serve, fill a glass with ice, add a cucumber slice or two, and cover with lemongrass-infused water. Garnish with a blade of lemongrass, and enjoy.

CHAPTER SEVEN

SHAKER MEDICINAL HERB GARDEN

The American Shakers, a religious sect founded in the 1770s, have made an enduring mark on our culture, through their high-quality craftsmanship (particularly furniture, which is much valued to this day), music, architecture, and agriculture. The early Shakers used the most current methods of the day to produce the best medicinal herbs and highest quality seeds for American gardens.

Shaker villages, most located in New England, were religious communes; multiple families lived together. Known then as the United Society of Believers in Christ's Second Coming, they were called Shakers for their religious fervor—expressed through "shaking" whenever the spirit moved them during worship.

The garden in this chapter is an homage to the Shakers, whose tidy raised beds produced all the food and medicinal herbs their communities needed.

Shakers believed that the state of your garden reflects the state of your soul and that gardening is a way to exercise the spirit. The messier the garden, they felt, the messier the soul. The Shakers strove for excellence. From seeds to dried herbs to oils and ointments, they provided remedies that were prescribed by the doctors of the day. Today Shaker communities have all but disappeared, mainly because of their opposition to marriage and rejection of sex as a sin (policies that weren't very sustainable over the long run), but their legacy lives on.

Now, more than two centuries later, with a growing movement in America for eating locally sourced produce, it is worth revisiting Shaker practices, as we form new models for sustainable food sources and a sustainable economy.

THE MEDICINAL HERB GARDEN

You will plant this easy-to-grow perennial garden once and tend it year after year. The herbs can be used medicinally, fresh or dried, in teas, and the flowers can be used as bouquets or as a fragrant garnish for formal meals. All the plants in this garden are drought tolerant and will survive on the natural rainfall in most areas. In a few years, the plants can be divided and used to colonize new areas, or you can recoup gardening expenses by selling, donating, or trading the plants.

What to Plant

In this garden, you'll plant Echinacea, Feverfew, Lemon balm, Hyssop blue, Yarrow, Lavender bergamot
Difficulty level Easy
Zones 4–9
Sunlight Full sun to partial sun
Earliest planting date Six weeks before the average last spring frost date

Maintaining the Garden

You'll soon discover that none of the perennial herbs in your garden are prone to disease or attract pests. In fact, what they do attract is an army of honeybees and bumblebees, butterflies, ladybugs, and other wildlife that are beneficial to the garden and the environment. The presence of these insects means you are doing things right. This is what organic gardening is all about—a way to join the natural world and benefit from all that nature has to offer.

Echinacea
seed or seedling
1 per 1 sq. ft.

Feverfew
seed or seedling
1 per 2 sq. ft.

Lemon Balm
seed
1 per 4 sq. ft.

Hyssop Blue
seed
1 per 1 sq. ft.

Yarrow
seed
1 per 1 sq. ft.

Lavendar Bergamont
seed
4 per 1 sq. ft.

Starting a Medicinal Herb Garden from Seed, Outside

Start this bed by directly sowing the seeds outdoors in a raised bed. Sow the seeds in the fall, starting two weeks after the first frost; for the herbs to germinate, they need a minimum of six weeks of cold weather—40 degrees or colder—before a period of warmth. If you start the seeds too early in the fall they may begin to germinate and won't have enough time to grow before the cold kills them.

You can also sow the seeds in early spring, starting eight weeks before the average last frost date. After eight weeks, you can jump-start the process by watering the garden deeply and covering the raised bed with a hoop house; it will create a moist environment so you won't have to water the seeds very often, but make sure that the soil is kept moist until they start to germinate.

You can also let nature take its course and allow the seeds to germinate when the climate is right. Once you've reached the last spring frost date, keep the soil moist until the seeds germinate, then water deeply as needed.

Starting a Medicinal Herb Garden with Transplants

It's also easy to grow medicinal herbs indoors and transplant the seedlings outside after the last spring frost. You can purchase seedlings or start them yourself from seed. Because all of the medicinal herbs in this garden are cold-hardy, self-sowing plants, you can winter-sow them in containers in early winter and they will germinate in the spring. (See page 46 for instructions.)

Saving Seeds

Saving medicinal herb seeds is easy. First, allow some of the plant to flower by not harvesting it. When the plant flowers, allow the flower head to mature into a seed head. Allow the seed heads to dry out on the plants. Once they are dry, carefully prune off the seed heads and place them in a paper bag. Take dry seed heads inside and separate the seeds from the rest of the plant. Place the seeds in labeled paper envelopes or Ziploc bags and store them in a dry, cool, dark place until spring.

GROWING MEDICINAL HERBS

You can start this bed from seeds, outside, or from transplants purchased from your local gardening center. Here are few steps to take to keep everything in balance so you won't have to work too hard in the garden:

1. Once the plants are at least 4 inches high, water the garden deeply, weed and mulch the plants, and water again.

2. Prune dead leaves and branches throughout the growing season.

3. Water deeply when there is a drought in your area.

4. Starting in the fall of the garden's second year and every fall after that, you will need to divide the herbs. This will keep the plants from growing out of control and crowding each other.

5. All of the plants in your herb garden are invasive, and if they're allowed to go to seed and self-sow, you'll have medicinal herbs growing everywhere. Harvest herbs regularly and before they flower and go to seed.

6. If you would like to save some seeds, allow at least one of each herb plant to flower and go to seed.

CONTAINER & RAISED-BED GARDEN PLANS

WHAT YOU NEED

- 18-gal. galvanized container
- Gravel or filler for proper drainage
- Organic potting soil
- Plants

You don't need to put all the plants in your container garden at once; you can buy some plants and start others from seed—or from plants you've started indoors.

Container Plan

Container Garden Plan: 18-gallon Container

A container planted with medicinal herbs is both beautiful and useful.

Plant one of each of the plants shown in "What to Plant," on page 109. You'll love the stunning display of white, yellow, blue, and purple flowers. Clip off the spent flowers to keep the blooms coming.

PREPARING THE CONTAINER

1. Make at least 20 drainage holes in the bottom of the container using a ¼-inch by 3-inch nail and a hammer.

2. Fill the bottom of the container with a 2-inch layer of ¾-inch gravel or a lighter substitute.

3. Add organic potting soil to fill the container up to 2 inches from the top. Water thoroughly.

STARTING FROM SEED IN A CONTAINER

This container garden can be started from seed as early as eight weeks before the average last frost date in your area. Use any container you like as long as its capacity is at least 18 gallons.

After preparing the container, sow seeds according to the diagram and gently push them into the soil. Keep the soil moist and water it when necessary. Once the seeds germinate, mulch and water as needed.

STARTING WITH TRANSPLANTS IN A CONTAINER

When there is no longer a chance of frost at any time during the growing season, you can start your container garden with seedlings. Once you start planting, water the plants thoroughly, mulch, and water again.

MAINTAINING THE CONTAINER GARDEN

Container gardens tend to dry out quickly, so make sure there is adequate water for the plants to grow. Prune off any dead or yellow leaves whenever you see them, and if crowding occurs, divide the herbs. You can leave this container outside all winter. In the spring, when conditions are right, the plants will begin to grow again.

Medicinal herbs work well in a window box too. Plant them according to the diagram below.

Raised-Bed Garden Plans

There's so much history and tradition associated with medicinal herbs. Very early in human history, people who were knowledgeable about medicinal plants were leaders in their communities. Medicinal herb gardens have always been popular, not only for their practical uses, but for their beauty and fragrance as well.

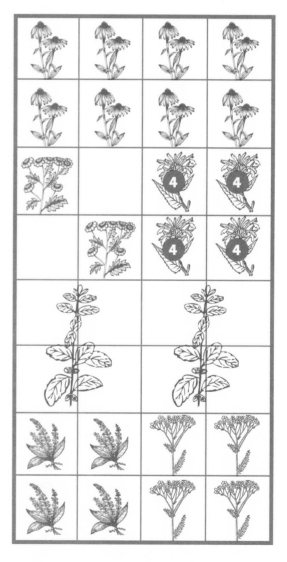

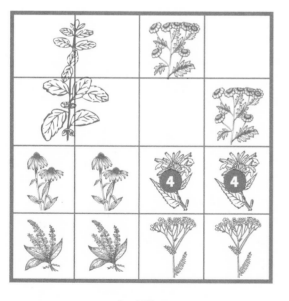

4 x 4 Plan   4 x 8 Plan

ECHINACEA
(Echinacea purpurea)

This native perennial, also known as Purple Coneflower, is a glorious garden plant that grows 24 to 36 inches tall, and sometimes even taller. It has a long blooming period, starting in the summertime. Echinacea grows large purple flowers that look similar to daisies. This drought-tolerant herb is a must in a summertime bouquet. Echinacea flowers attract wildlife like bees, butterflies, and other essential garden pollinators.

Height 24–36+ inches

In bloom Summer through fall

Seed to table 60–90 days

Spacing for seeds and transplants 1 per square foot

Native to North America

HARVESTING ECHINACEA FOR MAKING MEDICINAL TEAS

Harvesting Flowers and Seeds Prune flower heads just below the first set of leaves and allow them to dry thoroughly in a dehydrator, or spread the flowers on a tray, cover them with paper towels, and keep them out of sunlight, in a dark place, until you're ready to use them. You'll know when the flower heads are dry when the leaves crumble to the touch. Store dry flower heads in glass jars in a cool, dry, dark place for up to one year.

If you want to collect seeds, leave some of the flowers on the plant and allow them to go to seed, then prune the flower heads, separate the seeds from the heads, and place the dry seeds in a paper or Ziploc bag. Store them in cool, dry, dark place until next spring.

Harvesting Roots You can begin harvesting echinacea roots once the plants have been established in your garden for two to three years. It's easy to pry the roots out of the soil in single clump. Dig all the way around the base of the plant with a small hand spade. Gently shake off and remove as much of the soil as possible around the roots and wash them with water, making sure the hose is on low pressure. Then divide the root clump and replant some of the echinacea in the

CAUTION: The information in this chapter is not meant or implied to be a substitute for professional medical advice, diagnosis, or treatment, and is for general information only. Make sure to consult a doctor before using herbs.

garden. Be sure to water the soil thoroughly. To preserve the roots for later plantings, cut the stems off the remaining root clump and chop them into 1-inch pieces. Using a dehydrator, dry the roots for 24 hours or until they're thoroughly dry.

MAKING ECHINACEA TEA

To make echinacea tea, use 1–2 teaspoons of dried or 2–4 teaspoons of fresh echinacea flowers, leaves, stems, or roots per cup of water. Allow whatever part of the plant you're using to steep in a teapot in boiling water for 15–20 minutes. Then strain the echinacea and pour the tea into a cup. You can sweeten the tea, if you like, with honey, fresh stevia leaves, or raw agave nectar.

FEVERFEW

(Tanacetum [Chrysanthemum] parthenium)

This perennial medicinal herb is part of the chrysanthemum family. It's easy to grow, and once it blooms in spring, it doesn't stop. You can use the versatile leaves and flowers of this prolific plant to make a healing tea or a fragrant summertime bouquet. Feverfew has been used in Chinese medicine for millennia to reduce fevers and help with headaches and digestive ailments.

A bushy, popular herb, feverfew was used as a filler plant in cottage-style Victorian flower beds and gardens.

Feverfew can be at your service at any time throughout the growing season. Simply prune off enough flowers and leaves to make tea for immediate consumption, or harvest more to dry and use later in the winter. During the growing season you can chew on a few leaves to relieve a headache, or steep 4 tablespoons of fresh feverfew (leaves, stem, and flower) per cup of boiling water for 10 minutes. Then strain and drink the tea.

You can also dry the entire plant and use it to make tea. Steep 2 tablespoons of dried feverfew per cup of boiling water for 10 minutes. Strain and drink the tea.

Height 18–24 inches
In bloom Late spring through fall
Seed to table 50-60 days
Spacing for seeds and transplants 1 per 2 square feet
Native to North America

LEMON BALM

(Melissa officinalis)

Of the many herbs in the mint family, one of my favorites is lemon balm because it is fragrant, easy to grow, and makes a delicious hot or iced tea with a lemony twist by itself or mixed with mint and other herbs. You can also add cool lemon balm tea to ice-cold lemonade for a particularly refreshing drink.

Medicinally, lemon balm helps with insomnia or an upset stomach; it promotes longevity and reduces anxiety, and if you crush a few fresh leaves and apply them to your skin, it is effective as a mosquito repellent. It also has antiviral and antibacterial properties and is great for an all-natural lip balm; oil made from lemon balm is popular in aromatherapy. Commercially, lemon balm is used in toothpaste.

It's a great perennial to grow in containers and has many culinary uses, especially as a seasoning for meats and fish. It's also delicious in ice cream and fruit salads.

Lemon balm is one of my first go-to herbs when it starts growing every spring. You'll have plenty of lemon balm in no time. Small flowers grow throughout the stem, rather than at the top; trim them often and you'll still get plenty of flowers and seeds to save for later use.

Height and width 18–32 inches by 24 inches

In bloom Summer–fall

Seed to table 50–60 days

Spacing for seeds 1 per 4 square feet

Spacing for transplants One 4–6' container per 4 square feet

Native to Southern Europe and the Mediterranean

HYSSOP BLUE

(Hyssopus officinalis)

This perennial medicinal herb is a big help during flu season. The plants yield beautiful blue, small, edible flower spikes that grow to about 2 feet tall. I love the way they look in the garden. The medicinal properties of hyssop blue, when it's used as a tea, include relief of indigestion and lung congestion.

When it is used externally, hyssop blue is thought to speed up the healing of skin ailments because of its antibacterial properties. A member of the mint family, hyssop blue makes a relaxing tea, combined with lemon balm, to help ease a cough or cold. Even though it is a perennial plant, you'll need to re-seed every few years for a continuous harvest. Hyssop blue seeds can take up to 30 days to germinate from seed, so it's a good idea to use transplants from a local nursery or garden center.

Height 18–24 inches

In bloom Midsummer through fall

Seed to table 90 days

Spacing for seeds 1 per square foot

Spacing for transplants 1 plant per square foot

Native to Eastern Mediterranean and Asia

YARROW
(Achillea millefolium)

This medicinal perennial herb is easy to grow and comes in many different varieties. It is a drought-tolerant native of North America, and its flowers come in an amazing array of hues. Yarrow is a fragrant addition to summertime bouquets and dried-flower arrangements. It is easy to start in your own garden, from either seed or transplants, and it will thrive if you frequently cut off clusters of 10 to 20 tiny flowers.

Native Americans used yarrow to help with headaches, reduce fevers, and get to sleep. It is most commonly available with yellow or white flowers; its foliage can vary from lime-green to silvery gray, fernlike leaves.

Height 18–24 inches

In bloom Late spring through fall

Seed to table 90 days

Spacing for seeds 1 per square foot

Spacing for transplants 1 plant per square foot

Native to North America

LAVENDER BERGAMOT

(*Monarda fistulosa*)

This prolific medicinal herb is a fragrant perennial used for aromatherapy; its citrus scent is said to soothe the soul. A member of the mint family, lavender bergamot can be used in refreshing summertime drinks, sprinkled in salads, and used medicinally in teas to relieve a sore throat.

The lovely lavender leaves can be used fresh or dried in teas to ease a winter cold, and the flowers make a beautiful addition to bouquets and other floral arrangements.

Lavender bergamot is at its strongest and tastiest—and it is best to use it—before the herb flowers. And it will flower, as it should be allowed to do, all summer long.

Height 24–36 inches

In bloom Late spring through fall

Seed to table 60 days

Spacing for seeds 4 per square foot

Spacing for transplants 1 plant per square foot

Native to North America

USES FOR MEDICINAL HERBS

MEDICINAL HERB	MEDICINAL USES	HOW TO USE
Echinacea	Boosts the immune system to prevent the common cold or flu.	Tea
Feverfew	Helps relieve migraines as well as fevers, minor pain, . and inflammation.	Tea
Lemon balm	Great for soothing upset stomachs and as a mosquito repellent. Helps relieve minor cuts, burns, and mosquito bites.	Tea or Poultice
Hyssop blue	Helps with digestion and lung congestion associated with a cold or cough. Helps to heal skin.	Tea or Poultice
Yarrow	Helps reduce fevers, headache, and menstrual symptoms, and can be used as an astringent and sleep aid.	Tea or Poultice
Lavender bergamot	Helps to soothe a sore throat.	Tea

RECIPES FOR SHAKER MEDICINAL HERBS

Flu Season Relief Tea

Makes about 1 cup

Warm tea always makes me feel better, and this lemon-flavored tea definitely hits the spot.

> 1 tbsp. dried lemon balm and 1 tbsp. dried bergamot
>
> or
>
> 2 tbsp. fresh lemon balm and 2 tbsp. fresh bergamot
>
> 1 cup of water

Seep dried or fresh lemon balm in boiling water for 10 minutes, then strain and add a few drops of fresh lemon juice. Sweeten the tea with honey or fresh stevia leaves.

Medicinal Herb Poultices

Makes about ¼ cup of medicinal paste

Herb poultices are a great natural way to help heal minor cuts and skin inflammations and to relieve mosquito and other insect bites.

> Collect 1 cup of fresh leaves from herbs
> such as lemon balm, hyssop blue, or yarrow.

Using a mortar and pestle, mash the herbs into a paste. Spread the paste on a bandage or sterile gauze pad and place it on the affected area. When the paste dries out, replace the poultice.

Healing Salves & Moisturizing Balms

Makes either 3 or 4 cups

Here's a great way to use infused herbs to make two classic skin treatments. *Balms* are medicinal ointments that have the consistency of lip balm and that are used to soothe skin irritations such as rashes and burns. *Salves* are healing ointments that are more liquid in consistency than balms, but just as soothing.

2   cups infused herb oil (see facing page)

1   cup grated beeswax

Metal containers to store the salves

Using a double boiler, warm the infused herb oil. Add the beeswax little by little, and stir until all of the beeswax is melted. Pour into metal jars. Allow them to cool, then cover. To make balm, repeat the process above, using 2 cups of grated beeswax, which will make the solution thicker.

Infused Herb Oil

Makes 6 ounces

A good way to extract the benefits of herbs is to infuse them in oils. Essential oils are basically a concentrate of the herbs and must be diluted before use. These oils are very strong and are poisonous unless they are diluted. Infused herb oils can be used safely, however, as a salve or a lip balm, for example.

8   oz. olive oil
    (or almond oil, if you don't have a nut allergy)

1   eight-oz. jar

    Fresh herb or herbs of your choice,
    enough to fill the jar

    Cheesecloth on standby for later use

    Spoon

Harvest herbs when they are at their most potent (before flowering) and at the hottest time of the day. Harvested leaves must be dry to avoid mold, so don't harvest them if it has rained in the last 48 hours or if you watered the garden that morning. Separate the leaves from the stems and chop the herb leaves coarsely. Fill the jar to the top with the herbs. Fill the jar with olive oil and mix it with a spoon. Cover the jar with a lid and let it sit in a warm, sunny spot for six weeks. Then strain the mixture into a bowl, using a piece of cheesecloth. Squeeze the herbs as much as you can to release the oil. Place the oil back in the jar, and store it in the pantry for six months to a year.

CHAPTER EIGHT

VEGAN RAW GARDEN

Eating fresh, healthy, organic food can cost a lot of money these days, yet many people are opting for a vegetarian diet because of the health benefits, which include protection from some chronic diseases. Others are choosing to eat a vegan diet, which is entirely plant-based and cholesterol-free, because it excludes dairy products. And a growing number of people are moving toward a diet that reaps the maximum nutritional benefits from eating raw vegetables, which lose much of their nutritional value when they're cooked.

In order to follow through with any of these health-conscious lifestyle choices, you need access to lots of fresh vegetables. The vegan raw garden is composed of all the basic foods that many vegetarians eat daily, and it can provide an extended harvest of fresh vegetables—a raw-foodie's dream.

Whether or not you're a vegetarian, it's healthy to take a break from eating cooked foods and meat at least once a week. You can start by preparing a few entirely raw-food dishes for individual meals during the course of the week and then work your way up to a whole day of raw food. Growing vegetables in your own raised bed makes this easy to do.

My daughter and I love making salads fresh from the garden. I slice the cucumbers, and she breaks apart the lettuce leaves. Then we mix all the ingredients together with our favorite vinaigrette. It's fun, the result is fresh, and your kids will be ready to eat it.

I was first inspired to create a vegan raw-vegetable bed when my husband went on a strict salad-and-meat diet for lunch and dinner. He lost 25 pounds. If your goal is to lose weight, there's no better way than to work in the garden and grow the healthy food you need to eat.

THE RAW GREENS GARDEN

You'll be able to start the vegetables in this chapter from seed, right in the garden, for less than $20. With its crisp, colorful assortment of vegetables and lettuces, your vegan raw garden will inspire salad making all season long. I've included the easiest edibles to grow to help make eating a healthy diet feel like second nature. This garden plan is also designed to put a rainbow of multi-colored, nutrient-dense greens on your plate.

To extend the harvest in this garden, I stagger it, sowing half the seeds right in the garden starting six weeks before the average last spring frost date, and then covering it with a hoop house. Four weeks later, I sow the other half of the garden. Once I've eaten the first crop of harvestable greens, another crop is close behind, and I keep sowing more seeds until early summer. In late summer, I repeat the process until the average first fall frost date. It's my own never-ending salad bar . . . well, almost never-ending. Although every year I try to see how long I can grow food in the garden—I always have fresh, home-grown food on my Thanksgiving table—by Christmas, I have to give in. It's just too snowy and cold outside, and my hoop house can't provide the plants with temperatures that are above freezing.

What to Plant

In this garden, you'll plant Cucumbers, Celery, Spinach, Swiss chard, Kale, Mesclun mix
Difficulty level Easy
Zones All
Sunlight Full sun
Earliest planting date Six weeks before the average last spring frost

Garden Add-ons

Hoop house If you live in zones 3–8, protect your garden with a hoop house until average nighttime temperatures are in the 50s. (See pages 58 and 63 for more information about hoop houses.)
Trellis To find out how to build a simple trellis, see page 64.

PLANTS YOU NEED

Cucumbers
seed or seedling
2 per 1 sq. ft.

Celery
seed or seedling
4 per 1 sq. ft.

Spinach
seed
9 per 1 sq. ft.

Swiss Chard
seed or seedling
4 per 1 sq. ft.

Kale
seed or seedling
4 per 1 sq. ft.

Mesclun Mix
seed
16 per 1 sq. ft.

CONTAINER & RAISED-BED GARDEN PLANS

The Salad Bowl: A 12-Inch Container Garden

You can grow your own lettuces, even if you have just a balcony or a windowsill at your disposal. All you need is a container that is at least 12 inches in diameter. The container doesn't have to be very tall; a 4- to 8-inch-tall container is fine for this garden.

PLANTING THE CONTAINER

1. Cover the bottom of the container with a 1-inch layer of ¾-inch gravel or a lighter filler. Fill the container with organic potting soil. Water the soil, then sow your mesclun-salad-greens seeds. Here's how:

2. With your index finger, mark lines dividing the soil into 16 squares.

3. Place a pinch of salad seeds in the center of each square and lightly press the seeds into the soil. Don't press them into the soil too deeply. Mesclun-salad-greens seeds and most lettuce seeds need to be planted only ¹/₈ inch deep.

4. Since you've already watered the soil, you're all set. Within a few days the seeds will start to sprout, and within a few weeks you'll be harvesting fresh greens.

CONTAINER GARDEN MAINTENANCE

1. Place the container by a sunny window, or outside on a balcony or patio that will receive a minimum of 6–8 hours of direct sunlight per day.

2. Make sure you keep the soil moist until the seeds start to sprout, then allow the surface of the soil to dry out between waterings.

3. When the lettuce leaves are about 2 inches long, you can begin harvesting them.

Container Plan

4. A 12-inch container garden can provide enough greens for one person to eat from two to three times a week for up to three weeks. Plant one 12-inch container per person in your household and you'll have plenty of salad greens to go around.

5. Once you run out of lettuce you can re-seed the container.

Raised-Bed Garden Plans

Feel free to use this plan as a guide. If you don't like some of the recommended vegetables, plant more of the ones you do like. Planting lots of different things in a raised-bed garden keeps your meals interesting.

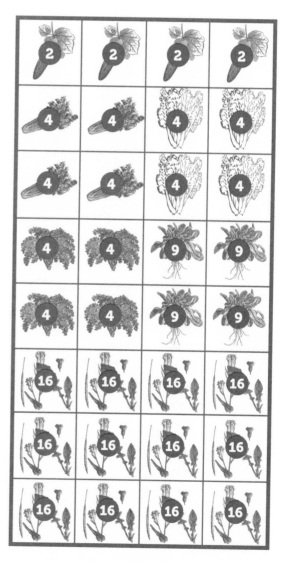

4 x 8 Plan

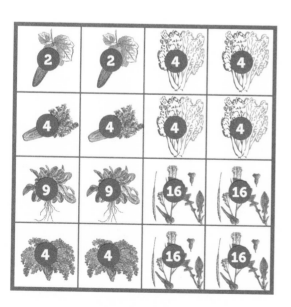

4 x 4 Plan

GROWING A VEGAN GARDEN

1. Start this bed as early as six weeks before the average last spring frost. Water the soil before sowing the seeds.

2. For a staggered harvest, first sow half the bed; four weeks later, sow the other half.

3. Use a hoop house over the garden bed until average nighttime temperatures are in the 50s. Make sure seeds are moist until they germinate, and water and weed as necessary.

4. Once the celery, cucumbers, Swiss chard, and kale are 4 inches tall, weed and mulch around the plants.

5. Harvest baby greens when they are 2 inches tall. Remove dead leaves, and weed and water regularly. Once summer arrives and your lettuces and spinach have started to bolt (begun to flower), pull out the plants and leave the area unplanted until late summer. Then re-seed half the area.

6. In the fall, two weeks before the first fall frost date, sow the last of your lettuces or spinach, remove the cucumber vines and trellis, and cover the garden bed with a hoop house. Water and weed as necessary.

7. Harvest greens into winter until temperatures are no longer favorable. Note that many cold-weather crops will continue to grow as long as the ground isn't frozen and the microclimate (the temperature immediately around the plants) doesn't fall below the 50s at night. People living in zones 8 and 9 (see the hardiness zones chart on pages 26–27) can keep plants growing through the coldest winter days with a hoop house.

CUCUMBERS

I've grown more than fourteen kinds of cukes over the years. Cucumbers grow so abundantly in my garden that the family and I take them for granted at this point. Cukes are a great veggie to try if you're just beginning to garden, and they can be used in so many ways.

For a fall harvest of these wonderful veggies, plant a new crop in mid- to late summer.

Farm-grown cucumber vines grow along the ground and require a lot of space. You can maximize the space you have by weaving your cucumber vines through a trellis, where they'll grow vertically. You'll notice the tendrils stretching out to coil around the trellis, attaching the vines to the wire and helping to support the vine when it's heavy with cukes. As the fruit forms from the plant's yellow edible flowers, gravity will kick in and you'll have super-straight cucumbers.

Seed to table 50 days
Spacing for seeds and transplants 2 per square foot
Native to Mediterranean and south Asia

Patti's Pick

Marketmore 76 (*Cucumis sativus*) This is the classic American cucumber, a great cool-weather variety, and perfect for salads and pickles. The vines are prolific, and the cucumbers grow to 8 inches or longer.
Height Vine can grow to 12 feet or more

PESTS & DISEASES

You can keep common pests and diseases at bay by weeding and removing any yellow or dead leaves, and treating pest infestations or diseases right away.

HARVESTING CUCUMBERS

Cucumbers are prolific growers, and you'll be able to start picking them right off the vine as early as 50 days after planting if you've started from seed—sooner if you plant seedlings. Each plant will yield about 10 cucumbers per vine over a five-week period before the vine's yield starts to slow down. Harvesting your cucumbers right before you eat them lets you enjoy all of their nutritional benefits.

SAVING CUCUMBER SEEDS

Allow at least one cucumber per vine to ripen past the point where you'd eat it before salvaging the seeds. You'll know the cucumber is ready for seed harvesting when it has lost its green color and is turning yellow to white.

1. Pick the cucumber and slice it down the middle. Scoop out the seeds, separate them from the flesh, and rinse them with water until all the flesh is gone from the seeds.

2. Spread out the seeds on a paper plate, a paper towel, or a paper bag, and allow them to dry in a cool dark place.

3. Once the seeds are dry, put them in an envelope or a plastic baggie and store them in a cool dark place.

CELERY

I love growing celery because it makes me feel like I'm an accomplished gardener, and it's a cool and crunchy treat in salads. Celery is nutritious and high in water content, fiber, and calcium. It's also considered a negative-calorie food, based on the energy it takes to chew it. Munch away!

Seed to table Leaves: 60 days; young stalks: 90 days; full stalks: 120 days

Spacing for seeds and transplants 4 per square foot

Native to Egypt and the Mediterranean

Patti's Pick

Red Celery (*Apium graviolens*) This unique celery is hard to find in the grocery store or at a farm stand, but you can purchase the seeds online and start them yourself. Using red celery is a great way to add both great flavor and beautiful color to your meals.

Height 18–24 inches

PESTS & DISEASES

You can keep common pests and diseases at bay by weeding and removing any yellow or dead leaves, and treating pest infestations or diseases right away.

HARVESTING CELERY

Since you're growing your own celery, you'll have plenty of leaves to clip off and use in salads or soups. Once they start to develop, you can harvest individual celery spears by cutting them off close to the base and leaving the rest of the plant in the garden to continue growing. You can also let the celery plant grow to its fullest and then harvest the whole plant by pulling it out of the ground and cutting off the roots.

SAVING THE SEEDS & MAKING CELERY SALT

To harvest celery seeds, allow one or two plants to grow, flower, and go to seed.

To make celery salt, fill a salt or pepper mill with a half-and-half mixture of sea salt and celery seeds. You can then use the mill for fresh-ground celery salt whenever you want it.

SPINACH

I love baby spinach in salads, so I had to include it in this garden bed. Not only can you make entire salads based on spinach, you can also add a handful to a mixed greens salad or create a sautéed spinach side dish.

Just sow the seeds right into the raised bed. They may take a little longer to germinate than other greens, but just be patient—you'll be picking baby spinach in no time. Contrary to popular belief, spinach is not high in iron, but it is high in vitamin A, calcium, and protein.

Spinach is a quick-growing, cool-weather crop and for maximum success should be started from seed right in the garden—not indoors.

Seed to table 45–50 days
Spacing for seeds 9 per square foot
Spacing for transplants One 4- to 6-inch pot per square foot
Native to Central and southwest Asia

Patti's Picks

America Spinach (*Spinacia oleracea*) This smaller-leaf American heirloom—so compact it is perfect for growing in small spaces—is absolutely delicious when eaten fresh.

Bloomsdale Spinach (*Spinacia oleracea*)   A classic crinkled-leaf variety, this spinach is great for cooking.

Blackbird Spinach (*Spinacia oleracea*)   This popular spinach variety is grown in Italy.
Height 9–12 inches

PESTS & DISEASES

You can keep common pests and diseases at bay by weeding and removing any yellow or dead leaves, and treating pest infestations or diseases right away.

HARVESTING SPINACH

You can start clipping off baby spinach leaves when they are 2 or 3 inches long, and the plant will to continue to grow. Spinach bolts (starts to flower and go to seed) in hot weather. When a spinach plant starts to grow a flower stalk, it's time to harvest it; let the plant lie fallow until you start your fall spinach crop.

For a fall harvest, sow spinach seeds ten weeks before the average first frost date in your area (see the chart on pages 26–27), and for a staggered harvest, sow more seeds two weeks later. To extend your harvest into winter, place a hoop house over the garden once night-time temps reach an average of 50 degrees.

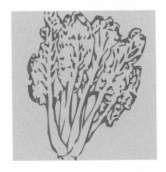

SWISS CHARD

This colorful veggie has had its ups and downs in popularity. It's so easy to grow that it's readily available at farmers markets, as is kale. Both leafy greens show up in community supported agriculture (CSA) boxes across the country with such frequency that it has created a backlash, in my opinion.

I've vowed to bring Swiss chard back into the conversation because it is so healthy for you (eating chard is known to help promote healthy vision) and looks beautiful on the plate. If you're a vegan or a vegetarian, lots of color and varying textures are important, because they are ways to know you are getting a complete meal and not a lot of just one or two components of a healthy diet. Because it thrives in the heat of summer, chard is a superb substitute for greens with less heat resistance, such as lettuce.

A relative of the red beet, this veggie's leaves are eaten raw or cooked. The seeds are easy to start in the garden. Just sow them where you want the chard to grow, starting six weeks before the average last spring frost date, and allow them to germinate under a hoop house.

Seed to table Baby leaves: 30 days; full-size leaves: 50 days
Spacing for seeds and transplants 4 per square foot
Native to Sicily

Patti's Pick

Rainbow Chard (*Beta vulgaris cicla*) This rainbow variety will give you red, white, yellow, and orange chard.
Height 12–32 inches

PESTS & DISEASES

You can keep common pests and diseases at bay by weeding and removing any yellow or dead leaves, and treating pest infestations or diseases right away.

HARVESTING SWISS CHARD

About seven weeks after planting you can start harvesting the colorful leaves from the outside of the chard plant—in spring, summer, and fall, and even beyond the first frost. To harvest Swiss chard, simply remove the outer leaves and leave the smaller inner leaves intact for future growth. You can remove the outer leaves by hand or with a pair of pruning shears.

KALE

You may not remember eating kale or buying it at the grocery store, but you have definitely seen it used as a garnish at buffets. Kale is a highly nutritious vegetable that needs to be part of your diet. I love eating it raw in salads, in hearty autumn soups, or prepared as a side dish, as an alternative to spinach. You can start eating kale about one month after planting it.

Seed to table Baby: 25 days; full-size: 40 days
Spacing for seeds and transplants 4 per square foot
Native to Mediterranean and south Asia

Patti's Picks

Lacinato Kale (*Brassica oleracea* var. *acephala*) This prehistoric-looking, large-leafed kale comes from Italy and has a delicious, strong taste.

Red Winter Kale (*Brassica oleracea* var. *fimbriata*) A cold-hardy, red- and green-leafed kale, it looks as beautiful on the plate as it does in the garden.
Height 9–12 inches

PESTS & DISEASES

Keep pests and diseases at bay by weeding and removing any yellow or dead leaves, and treating pest infestations or diseases right away.

HARVESTING KALE

Harvest kale in the early morning by cutting off the largest leaves. Allow the plant to stay in the ground and continue to grow. In the summer you may see kale plants wilt in the sun. If they don't bounce back around sunset, you may need to water them. Kale is cold-hardy, so you can plant more in the fall. If the plants are protected in a hoop house, you can continue the harvest through the winter.

MESCLUN MIX

This healthy salad mix comes from the south of France, where it is traditionally comprised of chervil, arugula, endive, and lettuce. Now mesclun is simply the generic name for any mixture of baby lettuces. The greater the variety of greens on the plate, the more enticing and healthier it is. Mesclun is the key ingredient in the vegan raw garden and will take up almost half of the beds.
Seed to table Baby leaves: 25 days; full-size leaves: 40 days
Spacing for seeds 16 per square foot
Spacing for transplants One 4- to 6-inch container per square foot.
Native to Europe

Patti's Pick

European Mesclun Mix This colorful, fast-growing mixture of European lettuces includes romaine, radicchio, arugula, endive, and others. The beautiful reds, purples, yellows, and bright greens in this healthy, tasty mix make them the perfect addition to any green salad. Many seed companies have their own version, or you can get the individual seeds for the lettuces you like and create your own mix. Sow half of your mesclun seeds in the garden first; then, for a staggered harvest, sow the rest four weeks later.

Height 9–12 inches

PESTS & DISEASES

You can keep common pests and diseases at bay by harvesting greens regularly, weeding, and removing any yellow or dead leaves, and treating pest infestations or diseases right away.

HARVESTING MESCLUN MIXES

Mesclun greens can be harvested and eaten in about one month, when they're about 2 inches long. Cut off the baby lettuce leaves with a pair of scissors without removing the whole plant. More leaves will continue to grow, providing you with salads over a period of weeks.

What could be more convenient? All you need to do is harvest what you want to eat, when you want to eat it. There's no need to store your lettuce in the fridge—Mother Nature takes care of that. Your veggie aisle is right outside your door.

EXTENDING THE HARVEST

If you shade the area where you are growing a mesclun mix in the summertime, you'll get more out of the harvest. Instead of plastic, cover a hoop house with a shade cloth and position it over the plants in order to keep them cool and out of direct sunlight.

Summer weather will give you a break from eating mesclun, since hot conditions are not conducive to growing lettuce. Instead, sow seeds for new plants in late summer to start up the salad factory again in the fall.

Cover the garden with the hoop house (covered with plastic) when the average nighttime temps are in the 50s, and keep harvesting healthy greens into winter.

HOW MUCH SHOULD I HARVEST?

Mixed greens or kale
1 cup will feed
one person

Celery
1 large spear
is enough for two

Swiss chard
1 cup, chopped,
is one portion

Cucumber
1 is enough for
four people

Spinach
a handful will feed
one person

RAW FOOD RECIPES

Cool Weather Mixed Greens Salad with Cucumber & Red Celery

Serves 6

This makes a delicious side salad in the spring. Add chicken, meat, or fish to the greens, and have a great meal.

1	cucumber, cubed, with peel on
2	red celery spears
4	handfuls of spinach
4	cups mixed greens
1	cup crumbled feta cheese (omit for vegan or dairy-free diets)
1–2	cups of any other vegetables available in the garden.

Place greens and vegetables in a large bowl and toss. Add the feta cheese, if you're using it. Mix the greens with the dressing of your choice and serve immediately.

Champagne Vinaigrette

Makes 1 cup

You can double the recipe for this versatile dressing and store it for up to a month in the fridge.

¼	cup champagne vinegar
1	shallot or bunching onion
½	cup olive oil
1	tbsp. aioli garlic mustard (see page 185)
2	tbsp. chives
1	garlic clove
	White pepper to taste

Puree the ingredients in a blender and store in a jar. Mix before using.

Cucumber Salad

Serves 4

When I was growing up, this salad was a favorite of mine, and it is very simple to make. It is the perfect, crisp summer side dish, especially for anything that's barbequed.

2	large Marketmore cucumbers
¼	cup white vinegar
1	handful chopped fresh dill
	Salt and pepper to taste

Peel the cucumbers and slice them down the middle. Using a spoon, scoop out the seeds. Slice into ¼-inch-thick pieces and place in a bowl. Add the remaining ingredients and stir. Serve right away or store in refrigerator for no more than 24 hours before serving.

Cucumber Curry Salad with Celery & Cilantro

Serves 4

This is a spicy, fresh side dish that even the pickiest eaters in your family will love. It's also a great way to show off some of the veggies you've grown.

½	cup olive oil
⅓	cup raw agave nectar
2	tbsp. curry powder
	Dash of cayenne pepper
	Juice of 1 lime
¼	cup chopped cilantro
¼	cup finely chopped bunching onions
⅓	cup finely chopped celery leaves
2	unpeeled cucumbers, cubed

In a large bowl combine and whisk the olive oil, agave nectar, curry powder, cayenne pepper, and lime. Add the herbs and veggies and mix. Keeps in the fridge for two days.

Quinoa Salad with Celery, Walnuts & Capers

Serves 6

You can make this quinoa salad as a side dish or add meat and make it into an entrée. It can also be use as filling, wrapped in large Swiss chard leaves, and served as an appetizer.

For the dressing

¼	cup olive oil
	Juice of one lemon
¼	cup white balsamic vinegar
2	cloves garlic
1	one-in. piece of fresh ginger root, peeled and minced
3	tbsp. agave nectar or honey
3	tbsp. goat-milk yogurt or soy yogurt (for vegans)
1	tbsp. capers

Mix ingredients for the dressing in a blender and store in a jar in the fridge. Mix before use. Dressing will last one week in the fridge.

½	cup red quinoa
½	cup white quinoa
1½	cups vegetable or chicken stock
½	cup chopped walnuts
4	celery stalks, thinly sliced
¼	cup chopped celery leaves
¼	cup chopped parsley
3	large fresh sage leaves, minced
1	scallion, minced
¼	cup capers
	Ground pepper to taste

Make the quinoa according to the package instructions, using vegetable or chicken stock. Combine all the remaining ingredients in a large bowl, then toss and dress to taste. Serve immediately or keep in the fridge for a few hours.

Homegrown Detox Drink

Makes about 16 ounces

This delicious vegetable juice will help flush toxins out of your system and give you more than your daily amount of fruits and vegetables. All you need is a juicer.

1	lemon, peeled
2	medium Granny Smith apples
1	two-in. piece of fresh ginger root, peeled
8	celery stalks and leaves
20	kale leaves
20	swiss chard leaves

Wash the veggies throughly. Starting with the lemon, juice the ingredients in the order given above. Once everything is juiced, skim off the foam, stir, and drink immediately.

Morning Cucumber Green Juice

Makes about 16 ounces, depending on the size and water content of the vegetables

The only equipment you need for this healthy summertime drink is a juicer. It's great for your digestion and gives you a jolt of nutrients to start the day off right.

1	lemon, peeled
4	medium Granny Smith apples
1	two-in. piece of fresh ginger root, peeled
1	cucumber, with skin on
1	tsp. raw agave nectar

Wash veggies thoroughly. Starting with the lemon, juice the ingredients in the order given above. Once everything is juiced, skim the foam from the surface, then stir in the raw agave nectar, and drink immediately. Ahhh . . .

CHAPTER NINE

MEDITERRANEAN VEGETABLE GARDEN

Mediterranean cuisine is all about fresh, seasonal cooking. Every region in the area has its own traditional dishes, so there are countless recipes to explore.

The Mediterranean diet is considered one of the healthiest in the world because of its focus on fresh ingredients—vegetables, olive oil, healthy fats, seafood, lamb, and goat. Doctors and nutritionists recommend the Mediterranean diet to their patients to help prevent chronic ailments such as heart disease and certain cancers. Recent studies have found that the Mediterranean diet also reduces the risk of developing Type 2 diabetes.

THE SUMMERTIME VEGETABLE GARDEN

Summer wouldn't be the same for my family without fresh, home-grown vegetables, and that's what this cuisine garden is all about. There are some finicky eaters in my household—namely, my husband and my daughter, who seems to follow his lead. For the life of me, I could never get either of them to eat eggplant (I believe they called it "super nasty") . . . until, that is, I started growing my own. Now they happily eat eggplant raw, in salads, and in other recipes.

The list of common Mediterranean vegetables is long, too long to grow all of them in one garden, so we are going to concentrate on traditional summertime vegetables from the Mediterranean that can be included in the widest range of meals and also serve as base ingredients for a plethora of others.

If you're surprised not to see tomatoes in this garden, don't worry! I haven't forgotten them. I feel so passionately about tomatoes that I've made them the centerpiece of Chapter Thirteen (pages 206–225), where you'll discover everything you need to know about growing and, best of all, enjoying tomatoes—whether you eat them fresh off the vine (nothing is better) or in the most delicious marinara sauce you've ever tasted.

What to Plant

In this garden you'll plant Eggplant, Dill, Basil, Pole beans, Zucchini
Difficulty level Intermediate
Zones All
Sunlight Full sun
Earliest planting date Four weeks after the average last spring frost date
Harvest Starting in 50 days

Garden Add-ons

Hoop house If you live in zones 3–8, protect your garden with a hoop house (see pages 58 and 63) until average nighttime temperatures are in the 50s.
Beanpole This is an easy-to-make support for staking up beans.

PLANTS YOU NEED

Eggplant
seed or seedling
1 per 2 sq. ft.

Dill
seed or seedling
1 per 1 sq. ft.

Basil
seed
4 per 1 sq. ft.

Pole Beans
seed or seedling
4 per 1 sq. ft.

Zucchini
seed or seedling
1 per 4 sq. ft.

CONTAINER & RAISED-BED GARDEN PLANS

Container Garden Plan

Any large container will work well for this garden. To give your patio a Mediterranean feel, use terra-cotta clay pots to grow your vegetables.

PREPARING & PLANTING THE CONTAINER GARDEN

Add a 2-inch-thick layer of gravel in the bottom of the terra-cotta pot, then fill it with soil that is rich in organic compost. Plant the container according to diagram, then water the soil thoroughly.

MAINTAINING YOUR CONTAINER GARDEN

You're going to need to water the container almost every day, except on rainy days. Check it regularly to see if the soil has dried out. The best way to maintain the right amount of moisture in the soil is to use a drip irrigation system (see page 16). Use a liquid fertilizer weekly, and add a generous handful of compost monthly as a mulch.

TIPS FOR USING TERRA-COTTA POTS

• Terra-cotta pots tend to dry out rather quickly, so use organic compost because it retains moisture and is packed with nutrients. You'll still need to pay special attention to these containers and make sure they are well watered.

• Terra-cotta pots are not weatherproof, like plastic pots or metal containers. The pots are made from clay and can easily crack once it gets below freezing outside. To safeguard your terra-cotta clay pots for the next growing season, empty out all the soil in the fall and store the pots in a basement or garage, sheltered from the winter cold.

WHAT YOU NEED

• Large terra-cotta or other container
• Gravel or filler for drainage
• Organic compost
• Plants

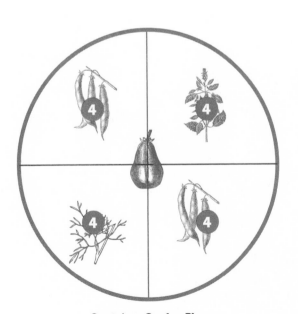

Container Garden Plan

Raised-Bed Garden Plans

If you have the space for it, a raised bed is the best way to grow a wider variety of Mediterranean veggies, while giving each plant enough room to develop to its fullest potential. You can follow these diagrams or replace some plants with your own personal favorites.

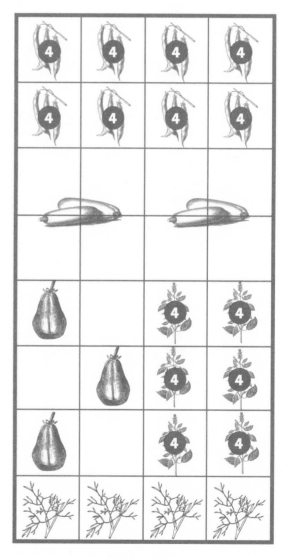

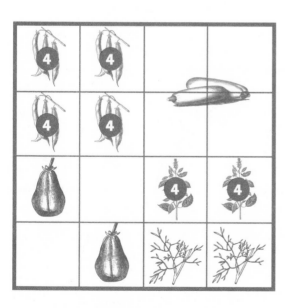

4 x 4 Plan

4 x 8 Plan

GROWING THE MEDITERRANEAN VEGETABLE GARDEN

1. You can plant beans, dill, basil, and zucchini from seed right in the bed. Eggplant seedlings should be planted in the bed at the same time. If average nighttime temperatures are in the 50s, cover this cuisine garden with a hoop house until nighttime temps are in the 60s.

2. Once the hoop house comes off, put in plant supports for your beans and eggplants. When the plants are at least 4 inches tall, water, weed, and apply a 1-inch-thick layer of mulch around the plants and water them again.

3. Water deeply two or three times per week, being careful not to water the leaves in order to prevent diseases and conserve water.

4. Weed the garden regularly. Prune and discard all brown or yellow and dead branches and leaves to prevent diseases. If you harvest vegetables regularly when they are ripe, your plants will continue to give you more to harvest.

EGGPLANT

Eggplant, a native of India, was introduced to the Mediterranean by the Moors in the early Middle Ages. Thomas Jefferson grew eggplants in his kitchen garden in 1809 and often shared them with neighbors.

Eggplant is a member of the nightshade family and is closely related to tomatoes, potatoes, and peppers. Eggplant leaves are not edible, but the skin of the fruit is.

A nutritious, versatile, summertime vegetable, eggplant can be prepared and eaten in myriad ways—raw, grilled, baked, or fried. Each plant will yield between five and ten eggplants throughout the growing season, so try as many recipes as you can. Eggplant is thought to have heart-healthy attributes and can reduce cholesterol. It's also a great source of folic acid and potassium.

Eggplant is an annual in zones 3 to 9, but it's a perennial in tropical climates (zone 10), where a plant can be fruitful for two or more years.

STARTING EGGPLANTS FROM SEEDS

If you live in the tropics (zone 10), you can start eggplant seeds directly in your garden bed. The growing season is long enough for the seeds to germinate and grow to maturity.

In all other climate zones, however, you'll need to start your seeds indoors six to eight weeks before the average last spring frost date. Eggplants can take up to 21 days to germinate, and need at least four weeks more to grow into a strong, healthy plant that you can transplant into your Mediterranean vegetable garden. You can also buy organic seedlings online or at your local garden center.

I find that I don't need many eggplants in my garden. For me growing multiple varieties is more important, so I often purchase organic heirloom eggplant seedlings instead of starting them indoors, where they take up too much room in my seed-starting area. I like to grow between five and seven varieties per year and no more than seven plants.

PLANTING EGGPLANT

1. Dig a hole in the center of the planting square and add a handful of soil acidifier. Eggplants like acidic soil.

2. Place the plant in the hole without disturbing the roots.

3. Fill the hole with soil, water, and mulch, then water the soil again.

4. Water frequently for the first four to six weeks while the plant establishes itself. Gradually allow the garden to dry out between waterings.

5. The plants can grow to over 4 feet tall. As the fruits develop, they'll weigh down the plant, so it will eventually need support; 6-foot wire cages work well. Place them over the plants when you first plant them.
Seed to table 70–85 days
Spacing for seeds and transplants 1 per 2 square feet
Native to India

Patti's Picks

Rosa Bianca Italian Heirloom Eggplant (*Solanum melongena* var. *esculentum*) This mid-size Italian variety is round and has variegated pink, red, and white skin.

Black Beauty Eggplant (*Solanum melongena* var. *esculentum*) A classic Italian variety, Black Beauties are great in eggplant Parmesan, caponata, and ratatouille.

Italian White Eggplant (*Solanum melongena* var. *esculentum*) This white variety is less bitter and tastes creamier than the Black Beauty and can be used in all of your favorite eggplant dishes.
Height 36–48 inches

HARVESTING EGGPLANT
You can start harvesting eggplant when the fruit is at least 4 inches long. If you want to save the seeds, allow the eggplant to slightly overripen before harvesting it.

SAVING EGGPLANT SEEDS
To save seeds from eggplants, remove the seeds from the slightly overripe fruit and spread them out in an even layer on a paper plate. Cover the plate with a paper towel and store it in a cool dark place until the seeds are thoroughly dry (in one or two weeks). Store the dry seeds in paper envelopes or in a glass jar in a cool dark place until it's time to start your garden again next year.

PESTS & DISEASES
You can keep common pests and diseases at bay by weeding and removing any yellow or dead leaves, and treating pest infestations or diseases right away.

DILL

Dill is an easy-to-grow culinary herb that is used fresh in many dishes. Harvest the green feathery leaves before the plant flowers in midsummer.

Dill is self-sowing and can be very invasive. Once dill starts flowering (the blooms are edible too) prune off the flowers before they go to seed. If you want to save the seeds, wait for the flowers to go to seed and dry out. Cut off the seed heads, separate the seeds, and store them in a jar. Dill seeds are edible as well. They're delicious eaten with cucumbers or used as a seasoning for making pickles.

Salmon or cucumbers, paired with fresh dill, are classic combos. Dill is also used in Greek and Scandinavian cuisine, among others.

STARTING DILL SEEDS

There's no need to start dill indoors. Once the danger of frost is past, sow a pinch of at least 10 seeds in the middle of each square foot on the surface of the soil. Pat them gently into the soil and water with a watering can. Keep the seeds moist until they germinate. Once the dill plant reaches 4 inches tall, weed the area, and mulch.

Keep the area weed-free and water regularly. Since dill is an herb you won't need to worry about pest or diseases.

Seed to table 70 days
Spacing for seeds 1 per square foot
Spacing for transplants One 4- to 6-inch pot per square foot
Native to Southeast Asia, India

Patti's Pick

Mammoth Dill (*Anethum graveolens*) Yes, it's big, and it has a bold flavor—perfect for vinaigrettes. This variety also adds fresh herb flavor and a nice texture to a garden salad.
Height 24–30 inches

PESTS & DISEASES

Pests and diseases do not affect herbs. Dill, for one, actually helps keep insect pests away by attracting predatory wasps and flies.

BASIL

The Mediterranean garden wouldn't be the same without the sweet scent of basil and its large green leaves. Basil is a wonderful companion for other vegetable plants, it's delicious in fresh Mediterranean meals, and it wards off garden pests like aphids. In cooler climates, through zone 8, basil grows as an annual and needs to be planted in the garden every year. In zones 9 and 10, it is a perennial; in those zones, continue to harvest basil and it will keep growing for years.

PLANTING BASIL

Plant four tiny pinches of basil seeds evenly spaced out per square foot. Moisture and warmth are crucial for basil to germinate, so if the seeds don't germinate right away, don't worry. Climate conditions just aren't there yet. Basil can take up to one month to germinate.

Once your basil seeds have sprouted, weed, water, mulch, and water again around the plants. Start harvesting basil by cutting off the top leaves when they reach between 8 and 10 inches tall, and keep harvesting. As with other herbs, basil tastes best before it flowers.

Seed to table 75–80 days
Spacing for seeds 4 per square foot
Spacing for transplants One 4- to 6-inch pot per square foot
Native to Southeast Asia, India

Patti's Pick

Large Leaf Italian Basil (*Ocimum basilicum*) This delicious, traditional basil has large, crumpled-looking leaves. Use it in anything—and everything!
Height 18–24 inches

PESTS & DISEASES

Pests and diseases do not affect herbs.

SAVING BASIL SEEDS

To save basil seeds, allow at least two of the plants to grow without harvesting so they can flower and go to seed. Once they've gone to seed and dried, clip off the spent flower head and separate the seeds. Store the seeds in a small jar until next year.

POLE BEANS

Pole beans play an essential role in the garden by providing nitrogen fixation—a natural process that helps keep your soil well fertilized and your plants healthy. Pole beans should be planted from seed and sown right in the garden, 1 inch deep, after the average last spring frost date.

Growing pole beans also maximizes growing space in your garden. All you need is a beanpole (see page 149 to learn how to build a tepee-style beanpole). Be sure to get your beanpole into the garden right away after sowing the seeds. Once they germinate, the plant's vines will quickly attach to the pole and continue to grow on it.

Once the bean seeds germinate and reach 4 inches tall, weed the area and mulch. When watering, be careful not to get the leaves wet. If any leaves turn yellow or brown pick them off and throw them away to prevent pests and diseases.

Everywhere you see a flower, there's potential for a bean pod to form. It's amazing to see how large the pods can grow—they can be as long as 12 inches. Pick pods when they are young and the beans inside haven't quite formed, and use them in salads. Pick medium-size pods for a great side dish. To save seeds, grow the pods to maturity and allow them to dry on the plant. Then pick them off, save some of pods for seeds, and use the rest in your cooking.

A low-calorie delight, beans contain vitamins A and C. Eat baby beans raw, or cook more mature bean pods before you eat them. Never overcook them. Beans taste better and retain more nutrients when they're still crunchy.

Seed to table 65–70 days

Spacing for seeds and transplants 4 per square foot

Native to Southern Mexico, Central America

Patti's Pick

French Pole Beans (Phaseolus vulgaris). This is a gourmet variety. Plant purple and green pods for a delicious-looking side dish or salad. Pick the pods when they are young and the beans haven't fully formed inside

Height: Vines grow up to 12 feet long

Spacing 5 per square foot

HOW TO BUILD A TEPEE-STYLE BEANPOLE

Pole beans are vining plants that need support from a structure, such as a trellis or pole, to grow properly and produce lots of healthy beans. A tepee-style beanpole is easy to make and does the job beautifully.

All you need are 10 thick bamboo stakes, at least 6 to 8 feet long, and some jute twine.

Using the twine, wrap the top of the bamboo stakes to create a tepee-like effect. Push the bottoms of the stakes into the soil as far as you can. Make sure they're firmly anchored in the soil—directly over the beans. The vines will climb up the bamboo stakes as they grow.

PESTS & DISEASES

Using disease-resistant seeds is the best way to prevent common bean diseases like bean mosaic disease or bacterial bean blight.

HARVESTING POLE BEANS & SAVING THE SEEDS

Beans harvestsed when they're young and small make a tender treat served raw in salads; once the beans have started forming in the pod, harvest them for cooking.

Harvesting often is key to keeping the plant flowering and producing beans for the whole growing season. For a staggered harvest, first plant half of the beans; then plant the other half four weeks later. To save bean seeds, allow some of the pods to continue to grow and dry on the plant. Harvest the pods, remove the dried beans from the pod, and store them in a jar in a cool, dark place until next spring.

Pole beans are self-pollinating, but if multiple varieties are planted next to each other they may cross-pollinate, so saving seeds won't ensure that the seeds are the same variety or a good seed to plant next year. In that event, just eat them and buy more seed next season.

ZUCCHINI

Zucchini is a stunner in the garden. It takes up a lot of room, but it is worth it. Although this variety of squash is native to the Americas, it has actually been cultivated for centuries by Italians; once it was introduced in Europe in the 1500s, the zucchini became a staple in Mediterranean cooking.

You can find zucchini in both vine and bush varieties. There's no need to plant multiple varieties, since no cross-pollination is required. The zucchini plant grows both male and female flowers, as most vegetables do. The female flower has a small fruit that forms below the flower; the male flower does not have a fruit.

The female flower is where the zucchini fruit eventually grows; make sure you don't pick too many of them so that there will be plenty of flowers later on to make one of my favorite recipes, Stuffed Squash Blossoms (see page 153). You may see blossoms fall off the plant regularly, but that's normal.

Once male flowers open and release pollen, they close and fall off the plant. Retrieve the blossoms and place them in your compost.

PLANTING ZUCCHINI

Starting zucchini plants from seed indoors is pretty easy, and you should have success starting them even if you've never started your own seeds. Start them the week before the average last frost date. Keep seeds moist until they germinate, which should be in five to seven days. You can start transplanting them outside starting four weeks after the last frost. You'll need to start squash seeds indoors if you have a short growing season.

An easy time-saver in warmer climes is to start the seeds right in your raised bed four weeks after the last frost. Start two seeds in a 4-square-foot area. If both germinate, remove one of the plants.

Seed to table 50–55 days

Spacing for seeds and transplants 1 per 4 square feet

Native to Italy

Patti's Pick

Stria di Italia (*Cucurbita pepo*) This is a bush variety that grows to an enormous size and needs a lot of room to grow.

Height 3 feet

PESTS & DISEASES

Most zucchini pests and diseases can be controlled by regular use of insecticidal soap. It's best to start a control program early, when plants are still young, to avoid any problems.

HARVESTING ZUCCHINI

Zucchini are best when picked early, starting at around 8 inches long. I sometimes pick a zucchini and start munching on it away right in the garden. The skin is thin and edible, and the flesh is soft and full of nutrients. As zucchini grow, the skin changes color and becomes thicker and harder and inedible.

Once zucchini start flowering, they will continue to flower and produce fruit until the plant dies.

If you want to save the seeds for next year, allow one zucchini to grow to maturity and become overripe. The fruit could be up to 3 feet long in some cases and will lose its vibrant color. Harvest the fruit and cut it down the middle. Scoop out the seeds, rinse them, and let them dry in a dark cool area. Place the seeds in a jar and store them until next spring.

RECIPES FOR A MEDITERRANEAN GARDEN

Babaganoush

Serves eight

This delicious recipe is so easy to make your kids will start making it on their own.

2	large eggplants
	Juice of 1 lemon
½	cup tahini (sesame paste)
4	tbsp. roasted sesame seeds
4	tbsp. crushed garlic
3	tbsp. olive oil
½	cup chopped parsley
¼	cup chopped garlic chives
	Freshly ground sea salt and ground pepper to taste

Preheat the oven to 400°F. Poke holes in the eggplants with a fork and roast on a greased cookie sheet or baking pan in the oven until the eggplant is soft and the skin is blackened, around 45 minutes. Allow the eggplant to cool and peel off the skin. Place the eggplant flesh and the rest of the ingredients in a bowl and mix by hand or puree in a blender. Serve at room temperature with Kalamata black olives and toasted pita triangles brushed with olive oil and sprinkled with ground sea salt. Babaganoush can be stored overnight in the fridge.

Pasta Primavera

Serves six to eight

Pasta and veggies make a healthy, fresh-from-the garden meal. This is one I'm always proud to serve. With so much color on the plate, I know my family is getting a healthy, balanced meal, and seconds are never a problem.

2	medium zucchini, cut into thin strips
2	Rosa Bianca eggplants, cut into thin strips
1	yellow bell pepper, cut into thin strips
1	red bell pepper, cut into thin strips
20	pole beans, 10 purple and 10 green
¼	cup olive oil
	Sea salt and freshly ground black pepper
1	lb. farfalle (bowtie pasta)
	Minced fresh dill
	Chopped fresh basil
½	cup chopped scallions
½	cup grated Parmesan cheese

Preheat the oven to 450°F. Toss all vegetables with oil to coat, and salt and pepper to taste. Place vegetables on a baking sheet and place in the oven for 10 minutes. Give the vegetables a stir and continue to roast them in the oven for 10 more minutes, then stir again and continue roasting until they start to brown. While the vegetables are in the oven, make the pasta. Don't overcook it—al dente is always best. Reserve 2 cups of the cooking liquid. In a large bowl, toss together all the ingredients, while they're hot, with the dill, basil, and scallions. Add freshly grated Parmesan cheese. Toss the veggies and herbs, and add the hot liquid little by little to moisten and combine with the cheese and olive oil. Serve with fresh Parmesan on the side.

Zucchini Bread

Serves six generously; makes 24 muffins

This fun late-summer and fall favorite is a great way to use some of the zucchini that can grow in great quantities in your garden. It's an easy recipe to make with the kids for a snack or family breakfast.

2	cups grated zucchini (4–6 small zucchini)
3	eggs
1	cup olive oil or vegetable oil
2	cups organic turbinado sugar
1	tsp. vanilla
2	cups white flour
1	cup wheat flour
1	tsp. salt
1	tbsp. baking soda
1	tbsp. cinnamon
1	tsp. baking powder

Preheat the oven to 350°F. Lightly grease two bread pans with olive oil. You can also make 24 muffins from this mixture. Mix the grated zucchini, eggs, oil, sugar, and vanilla together. Add the rest of the ingredients, starting with the flour and stir well. Pour the batter into the bread or muffin pans, and bake 50–60 minutes for bread or 25–30 minutes for muffins. Check for doneness by sticking a toothpick into the bread. If it comes out clean, the bread is done. If any batter sticks to the toothpick, continue to bake the bread. When it is done, the outside of the bread will be dark brown. Remove from the oven and cover with a clean cloth to cool. Remove from the pans, slice, and serve while still warm with butter or a sprinkle of sugar.

Stuffed Squash Blossoms

Serves five

Once you make these delicious cheesy bites—the best mozzarella sticks ever— you'll be clamoring for more squash-flower recipes, but don't use all of your blossoms or you won't have any zucchini left!

20	squash flowers
1	cup shredded mozzarella or fat-free ricotta cheese
2	tbsp. minced fresh dill
3	eggs
	Pepper, to taste
1	cup milk
2	cups flour

In the early morning, harvest the largest squash flowers from your garden, enough for 4 per person. Wash them well. Dry the squash flowers and keep them in the fridge until you're ready to stuff them. To make the filling, combine the cheese, dill, two of the eggs, and pepper in a bowl. To make the batter, mix the milk, the remaining egg, and flour. Remove the flower from the stem and stuff with the cheese and herb mixture. Twist the opening of the flower closed. Dip the stuffed blossom in the batter and fry until golden brown. Serve immediately with an herb pesto sauce or a warmed tomato marinara.

Italian Pasta Salad with Dill Vinaigrette

Serves eight

This raw dish is served cold—a favorite for family cookouts and beach picnics.

For the dill vinaigrette

½	cup bunching onions
¼	cup chopped fresh dill
4	tbsp. white wine vinegar
2	tbsp. aioli garlic mustard (see recipe on page 185)
½	cup olive oil
	Juice of ½ lemon

Place ingredients in a blender and mix. Store vinaigrette in a jar and shake before using.

For the pasta salad

12	oz. penne pasta, cooked
6	oz. fresh mozzarella cheese
4	tbsp. capers
1	red pepper, diced
1	yellow pepper, diced
1	small zucchini, diced
¼	cup green onion, finely chopped

Place pasta and fresh ingredients in a large bowl and mix. Add dill vinaigrette little by little and mix so that everything is coated. Chill in fridge until it's time to serve.

French Pole Beans with Garlic & Feta Cheese

Serves six

This classic side dish is a favorite on my dinner table.

½	lb. baby purple French pole beans
½	lb. baby green French pole beans
4	tbsp. olive oil
4	cloves garlic, minced
	Ground sea salt and ground pepper, to taste
	Juice of ½ lemon
1	cup feta cheese

Trim the ends off the beans, cover with about ¼ cup of water, and cook in a medium-size pan for 5 minutes. Drain the beans and return them to the pan. Add the olive oil and minced garlic to the beans and cook over medium heat, stirring often, for about 2 minutes. Remove beans from heat, add salt and pepper to taste, toss with lemon juice and feta cheese, and serve.

CHAPTER TEN

ONE POTATO, TWO POTATO, THREE POTATO GARDEN

Potatoes have had their share of ups and downs throughout their long history. On the positive side, for millennia potatoes fed the vast Inca Empire high in the Andes mountains, where they are native. On the negative side, in the middle years of the nineteenth century they were the major cause of famine in Ireland (touched off by potato rot) and mass migrations from that country.

According to the Cambridge World History of Food, potatoes are the fourth most important food on the planet. This versatile, tuberous plant, a member of the nightshade family, has spread and adapted to every continent, and each culture and cuisine has given it a unique spin.

There are few more popular homegrown vegetables in America than the potato, and if you follow the garden plans in this chapter, you'll be eating your own homegrown mashed potatoes at Thanksgiving dinner. Remember, while potatoes are highly nutritious and great for providing energy, they are also high in starches that break down quickly into sugars, which turn into fat if they're not used by the body. For people who have diabetes, the quick sugar rush provided by potatoes can be dangerous.

The way potatoes are processed to make French fries and potato chips doesn't help the situation much, but you don't have to give up these tasty foods altogether. There are healthy ways to prepare these mainstays of the American diet. You can start by growing your own potatoes. Most commercially grown potato crops have been sprayed with chemicals to keep them from sprouting, thus giving potatoes a longer shelf life. You can keep these harmful chemicals at bay—and out of your body— by growing your own. Of course, they'll taste more delicious, too.

HOMEGROWN POTATOES

Hardy and versatile, potato plants produce a lot of food in a small amount of space, and growing them is easy and fun. Potatoes are part of the nightshade family, like tomatoes and eggplants, but they grow in a very different way. They are started from seeds that look exactly like a potato and are planted 3–6 inches into the soil. All the potatoes you'll harvest from this garden grow above the seed potato.

To ensure a plentiful harvest, you'll need to start "hilling" soil around your potato plants when they're about 6 inches tall. Potatoes will form in the hills of soil, and it's important to keep them covered. See page 161 for all the details.

What to Plant

In this garden, you'll plant red, white, blue, and gold organic potatoes.
Difficulty level Easy
Zones All
Sunlight Full sun
Earliest planting date Four weeks before the average last spring frost

Garden Add-ons

Hoop House If you live in zones 3–8, protect your plants with a hoop house (see pages 58 and 63) until average nighttime temperatures are in the 50s (see the "Hardiness Zones" chart on pages 26–27).

MAINTAINING YOUR POTATO GARDEN

• Weed and water your potato garden regularly.
• It's easiest to pull weeds after watering; that's a good time to pull out any you can see, roots and all, so that they won't grow back.
• Once your potato plants are 8 inches tall, you can remove the hoop house and start hilling—mounding compost or straw—around the plants, leaving 2 or 3 inches of the plant above the mound. Keep hilling around the plants until the mound is about 18 inches tall.
• Continue watering as the plants grow. Weeds shouldn't be a problem.
• Tender "new potatoes" can be harvested six to eight weeks after planting. Mature potatoes will need a full growing season—between two and four months—to grow, depending on the variety.

PLANTS YOU NEED

Red Potatoes
seed potato
1 per 1 sq. ft.

White Potatoes
seed potato
1 per 1 sq. ft.

Blue Potatoes
seed potato
1 per 1 sq. ft.

Gold Potatoes
seed potato
1 per 1 sq. ft.

CONTAINER & RAISED-BED GARDEN PLANS

Growing Potatoes in Containers

If you don't want to devote a whole raised bed to potatoes, there are lots of other ways to grow potatoes in small spaces. For example, you can try using various kinds of grow bags, mesh wire, and even old tires and garbage cans. Nothing beats a container garden for high yield in a small space.

GROW BAGS

Potatoes don't need to be planted in the ground. They can be planted and grown in a bag! You can make your own grow bag out of burlap or weed cloth (also known as landscape fabric) or you can purchase an inexpensive plastic potato-growing bag at your local gardening supply store. Using a grow bag is easy.

1. Fill the bottom of the bag with 4 inches of soil.

2. Place 3–5 seed potatoes in the soil (see diagram, opposite).

3. Cover the seed potatoes with at least 4 inches of soil.

4. Water the soil regularly.

5. Once the potato plants have grown about 8 inches tall, add more soil or straw, up to 4 inches, burying the plants, and water the soil thoroughly.

6. Continue adding soil until the entire bag (or container; these instructions apply also to the containers described below) is full, up to 2 inches below the lip of the bag or container.

7. In about two months, see if you can pull out baby potatoes. After four months you should have full-size potatoes to eat.

MESH WIRE

1. You can also grow potatoes in a wire-mesh cylinder (just like the compost bin I showed you how to make in Chapter One (see pages 20–21 for instructions).

2. Place the cylinder in a sunny spot, fill the bottom with 4 inches of soil, and place seed potatoes on top of the soil.

3. Cover the seed potatoes with an additional 4 inches of soil and water the soil thoroughly, but not so much that you lose soil though the mesh holes.

4. Follow the growing and harvesting instructions above, under "Grow Bags."

TIRES

Using recycled tires is a variation on the grow bag.

1. Fill one tire with soil and plant potatoes as described above for grow bags.

2. Once the plants have grown enough to stick out of the top of the tire (by about 4 inches) add another tire and fill it with soil or straw.

3. Continue adding tires and filling them with soil or straw until the tire pile is about three to five tires high, depending on tire size.

4. Don't forget to water the soil regularly, as well as every time you add another tire.

5. Start harvesting baby potatoes after two or three months.

GARBAGE CANS

Another container I like for planting potatoes is a garbage can.

1. Use at least a 10- to 30-gallon garbage can made out of rubber or metal to grow between three and five potato plants.

2. Make drainage holes in the bottom of the garbage can and keep it slightly raised off the ground, using a few bricks or concrete blocks.

3. Follow the potato planting instructions above, under "Grow Bags."

Potato plants can grow just about anywhere dark. This diagram can apply to containers, tires, even garbage bags.

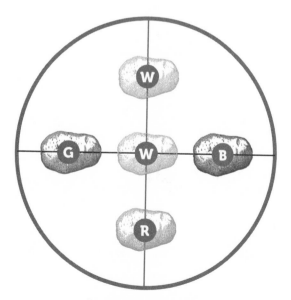

Container Garden Plan

Raised-Bed Garden Plans

Other than container gardens, raised beds are hands-down the easiest way to grow potatoes. For one, there's no digging, unlike with conventional gardens, and because they're so compact and easy to manage, raised beds consistently yield large potato harvests. You can also control the quality of soil in a raised bed—as well as moisture, which potatoes love—more than you can in a typical home garden.

All you need to know about spacing potatoes is this: plant no more than one potato plant per square foot. Mix and match colors and varities however you like.

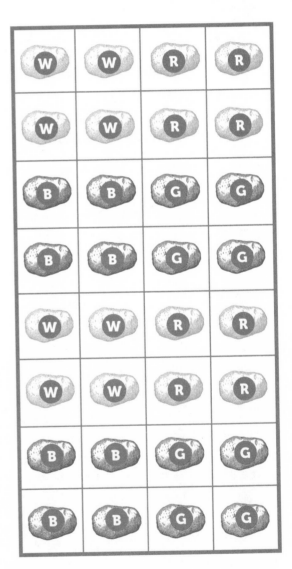

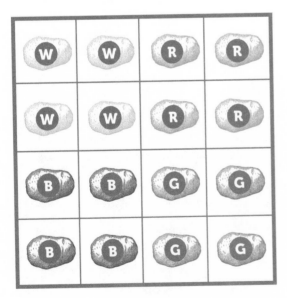

4 x 4 Plan

4 x 8 Plan

GROWING POTATOES

The most popular method of planting potatoes in small spaces is in raised beds. Growing a garden in a raised bed gives us control over soil conditions. Potatoes in particular need really loose, fluffy, well-tilled soil. They also like the soil pH to be slightly acidic.

1. Since you'll be hilling the potatoes, you want to begin with no more than 9 inches of soil in a raised bed, then deeply plant one seed potato every square foot, so your potato crop will have plenty of space to grow.

2. You can amend the rich organic soil in your potato garden by adding a soil acidifier. Potatoes grow best when the soil pH level is between 5 and 5.5. Starting out with a soil mixture of 50:50 or 25:75 topsoil to compost should give your soil a neutral pH level. To make the soil more acidic (or lower the pH), add 1 pound of elemental sulfur to a 4'x4' raised bed and 2 pounds of elemental sulfur to a 4'x8' raised bed. (For container gardens, use a handful of sulfur per seed potato.) Mix the sulfur into the soil well, and put a hoop house over your raised bed to start warming the soil. Let it sit for one month before planting the seed potatoes. Each raised bed will produce pounds of potatoes, so be creative and plant a variety of potatoes to keep your garden-to-table meals interesting.

3. Start planting four weeks before the average last spring frost. Small tubers can be planted whole, and large tubers can be cut in half before planting. Just make sure there are at least two eyes per piece. Plant one tuber per square foot, 6 inches deep. Water the soil and cover the garden with a hoop house. In less than a month potato plant sprouts will start cropping up.

PICKING THE RIGHT SEED POTATO

Of course you can buy potatoes at the grocery store and plant them—all of us did that experiment in grammar school—but to be a successful organic potato farmer, you want to start with an actual seed potato from a disease-free organic plant. One pound of seed potatoes usually contains between five and eight tubers. Every pound of seed you plant may yield up to 10 pounds of potatoes—quite an impressive ratio.

Buy and plant at least three different kinds of potatoes. It's great to try different varieties and see which ones produce the most in your garden. When the potatoes arrive, keep them in a cool, dark place. Two weeks before planting them, you'll notice that they've started to sprout, so place them by a window in the light to help the sprouts continue to grow.

Patti's Picks

Cranberry Red Potatoes (*Solanum tuberosum*) The red skin and flesh and fine moist texture of these early potatoes makes them particularly good when boiled for potato salad or sautéing.

BUY IT ONLINE

Organic seed companies that supply seed potatoes:

Seed Savers Exchange
www.seedsavers.org

High Mowing Organic Seeds
www.highmowingseeds.com

Seeds of Change
www.seedsofchange.com

Wood Prairie Farm
www.woodprairie.com

Abundant Life Seeds
www.abundantlifeseeds.com

Potato Garden
www.PotatoGarden.com

Elbas (*Solanum tuberosum*) Versatile and disease resistant, these white, late-yielding potatoes have excellent flavor—boiled or baked.

All Blue Potatoes (*Solanum tuberosum*) This is the most popular blue potato. A late-yielding, moderately disease-resistant variety, All Blues have deep-purple skin and flesh. Their rich, earthy taste adds an extra dimension to mashed potatoes; they're just as good roasted, steamed, or boiled. All Blue potatoes are high in antioxidants and minerals.

Yukon Gold Potatoes (*Solanum tuberosum*) These big, classic American yellow potatoes are perfect for baking and for fries and chips. They also store well.

Seed to table *Yukon Gold Potatoes* and *Cranberry Red Potatoes:* 70–90 days; *All Blue Potatoes* and *Elbas:* 110–135 days

Spacing for seed potatoes 1 per square foot

Height Up to 4 feet

Native to Peru

PESTS & DISEASES

Garden pests that can greatly reduce yield and even kill your potato plants include the Colorado potato beetle (which can also cause significant damage to tomatoes and eggplants) and slugs. If you have only one bed or a container of potato plants, you may be able to easily pick them off and squash them, but for larger infestations or a less bloody assault, try using organic sprays. The best defense against diseases is planting disease-resistant potato varieties.

HARVESTING YOUR HOMEGROWN POTATOES

Harvest new potatoes ten weeks from planting and mature potatoes 12–16 weeks from planting. Harvest new potatoes early in the season by carefully searching the soil with your hands as far down as you can and remove the small baby potatoes without disturbing the whole plant. Don't harvest them all. Leave most of the potatoes in the ground for the entire growing season.

Once the vines start to die back, the full-size potatoes are ready to be harvested and eaten. In the fall, just reach into the ground and take as many as you need, when you need them. Be sure to remove all the potatoes by the average first fall frost date. Store them in a cool, dark, dry place to prevent them from spoiling. Remember, as with tomatoes, the leaves of the potato plant are toxic and should not be eaten. Make sure you tell small children not to eat the leaves.

RECIPES FOR AN ORGANIC POTATO GARDEN

To narrow down the enormous list of my favorite potato recipes, I've chosen a few that include lots of ingredients from other cuisine gardens in this book, such as Asian greens, red winter kale, lemongrass, garlic chives, thyme, parsley, sage, and so much more.

Potato Salad with Edamame & Raw Walnuts

Serves six

Here's a potato salad with an Asian twist. New potatoes, like Cranberry Red, are particularly good in this salad. Take it to family events and be a star.

3	lbs. potatoes
6	strips of bacon
1½	cups minced bunching onions
2	cups chopped Asian greens
½	cup minced fresh cilantro
	Salt and pepper, to taste

For the Dressing

¼	cup finely minced lemongrass
2	cups mayonnaise made with olive oil
2	tbsp. agave nectar
3	tbsp. soy sauce
2	tsp. roasted sesame oil
½	tsp. hot mustard
	Salt and pepper, to taste

Boil potatoes whole with the skins on. Allow them to cool, then cut potatoes into wedges. Mix the dressing in a bowl. Add the dressing to the potatoes. Add the other ingredients little by little until all the ingredients are coated.

Crispy Baked Herb Parmesan Patriotic Potato Chips

Serves six

Once you get the hang of making these delicious potato chips, you'll want to make a lot of them. They're my favorite snack for Sunday football.

1	lb. Yukon Gold potatoes
1	lb. Cranberry Red potatoes
1	lb. All Blue potatoes
1	cup olive oil
2	tbsp. finely chopped fresh parsley or garlic chives
½	finely grated cup Parmesan cheese
	Salt and pepper, to taste

Preheat oven to 450°F. Wash potatoes well and slice them into 1/8-inch-thick pieces, using a mandolin. As you slice the potatoes, put them in a pot or bowl of water (to keep them from oxidizing and turning brown) until all are sliced. Drain the water and dry the potato slices. Brush the slices with olive oil and place them on a greased cookie sheet in one layer. Put the slices in the oven for about 9 minutes, turning them over halfway through the baking time. When each side is golden brown, remove the potato slices from the oven. In a bowl, toss the potatoes with fresh herbs, Parmesan cheese, and salt and pepper. Serve immediately.

MANCHEGO CHEESE

Manchego cheese (Queso Manchego) is made in the La Mancha region of Spain from the milk of Manchega sheep. It is a semi-firm white cheese with a nutty, sweet flavor (with hints of caramel), similar to a mild cheddar cheese.

Creamy Garlic Chive Mashed Potatoes with Manchego Cheese

Serves six

This is a tasty twist to a traditional dish you'll want to make and eat over and over again.

3	lbs. Yukon gold potatoes, washed, peeled, and quartered
3	tbsp. Earth Balance Buttery Spread (or 3 tablespoons unsalted butter)
1	cup grated Manchego cheese
3	tbsp. milk
¼	cup vegetable broth
	Ground sea salt and ground black pepper, to taste.
1	cup finely chopped garlic chives

Cover the potatoes with water in a pot and boil for about 15 minutes until tender. Strain the potatoes and put them back in the pot over low heat. Mash the potatoes and add the rest of the ingredients except the garlic chives. Use a hand mixer to cream the potatoes, adding more milk and butter as needed. Mix in the chives with a wooden spoon and serve with a generous pad of butter. Add a little more milk if you'd like a creamier texture.

Roasted Herb Potatoes

Serves eight

This is an easy side dish with a garden-fresh taste. Make these pota-toes for dinner and use the leftovers for breakfast.

1	lb. Yukon Gold potatoes
1	lb. Cranberry Red potatoes
1	lb. All Blue potatoes
3	tbsp. olive oil
	Salt and crushed black pepper, to tastel
½	cup parsley
½	cup chives

Preheat oven to 425°F. Cut the potatoes into 1-inch-thick wedges, place in large bowl, and mix with olive oil until the potatoes are lightly coated. Add salt and pepper and mix thoroughly. Make an even layer of potato slices on a lightly oiled baking sheet. Roast the potatoes for about 30 minutes until they are golden brown on the outside and tender on the inside. Flip potatoes once or twice while they are in the oven. Place the roasted potatoes in a serving bowl and toss with olive oil and herbs.

Triple Herb Potato Soup with Red Winter Kale & Manchego Cheese

Serves six

A classic combination, kale and potatoes pair deliciously in this recipe. Add a few generous gratings of Manchego cheese and you have a robust, fresh harvest soup that definitely hits the spot. It'll keep you healthy too. Kale is exceptionally rich in nutrients and health benefits, including cancer protection and lowered cholesterol.

3	tbsp. olive oil
1	cup chopped bunching onions
1	large elephant garlic clove, minced
10	leaves red winter kale, chopped
2	tender-crisp celery stalks and leaves, finely chopped
4	cups low-sodium vegetable or chicken stock
10	medium potatoes, peeled and cut into 2-in. pieces
1+	tbsp. Earth Balance Buttery Spread (or 1+ tbsp. unsalted butter)
6	strips low-sodium bacon, crumbled
1	tsp. dried thyme or 2 tsp. finely chopped fresh thyme
½	cup finely chopped fresh parsley, plus some for garnish
5	sage leaves, finely chopped
	Juice of 1 lemon
	Salt and pepper, to taste
	Manchego cheese, grated, to taste

In a large soup pot, sauté onions and garlic for 2 minutes in olive oil. Add kale and celery and sauté for 3 minutes. Add the vegetable stock and bring to a boil. Add potatoes and cook for 30 minutes until potatoes are tender. Take the pot off the stove and mash with buttery spread (or butter). Let cool. While the mixture is cooling, fry 6 strips of low-sodium bacon and crumble it into smallish pieces. Then combine the herbs, lemon juice, and salt and pepper in a blender. When the soup is warm (not hot), add the herb and lemon mixture to the soup and puree in a blender. Reheat soup and serve with grated Manchego cheese. Garnish with a sprinkle of finely chopped parsley.

Potato Latkes

Makes 24 latkes

Latkes are crunchy and comforting, just what you want in your tummy on a cold, rainy Sunday morning.

2	lbs. potatoes
1	egg, beaten
3	bunching onions, finely chopped
¼	cup matzo meal
	Salt and pepper, to taste

Preheat oven to 250°F. Wash the potatoes well and grate them with a fine cheese grater. As you grate the potatoes, place them in water to prevent them from turning brown. Drain the potatoes and squeeze out any remaining water with a clean dishcloth. Combine the grated potatoes with the rest of the ingredients in a bowl. Add a little more matzo meal if the potato mixture isn't binding together enough. In a skillet, fry the latkes in the vegetable oil, using 2 tablespoons of the potato mixture per latke, until they are brown on both sides, about 1 minute per side. Keep the latkes warm in the oven until it's time to serve them. Garnish with finely chopped onion and serve with apple-sauce and sour cream on the side.

CHAPTER ELEVEN

BERRY, BERRY GOOD GARDEN

I love growing edible perennials because I have to plant them only once—and then enjoy the fruits of my labor for years. In this cuisine garden bed, we're growing berries.

When growing edibles, especially fruit, variety makes it all worthwhile. Growing your own helps save money over the long run because your list of things to buy shrinks with every trip to the grocery store. Store-bought berries can be pricey, especially when they're out of season, because they've often traveled a long way to get to the market, and the cost of transportation is passed along to you. Even locally grown organic berries that you buy at a farmers market or supermarket can be expensive—another great reason for growing your own.

Blackberries, raspberries, and blueberries are native to North America, where they thrive. Luckily, few pests or diseases affect them. Maine is the largest producer of blueberries in the country, and the Pacific Northwest boasts a healthy blackberry and raspberry industry. These berries are a healthy treat too, especially because they are low in calories, high in antioxidants and fiber, and packed with vitamins. Consuming antioxidants is thought to reduce the risk of certain types of cancer, qualifying berries such as blueberries, raspberries, and blackberries as "super fruits," so feel good about eating as many as you want.

I love eating fresh berries in a fruit salad or on cereal, but you can also juice them, cook them, or preserve them by freezing or canning for later use in smoothies, jams, and jellies.

This garden wouldn't be complete without grapes. Fresh grapes make a healthy snack and are a great addition to a fruit salad. You can also make delicious grape jams and jellies to enjoy all winter. Grapes are vines, so they'll grow up a trellis and not take up too much room in the raised bed.

THE BERRIES & GRAPES GARDEN

With this versatile and easy-to-grow berry garden, you'll be doing your part to help save the planet, and you'll save lots of money as well, because your plants will continue to produce fruit for many years to come. Remember, though, that this is a perennial garden. You won't get much of a harvest (if any) the first year—it will take several years before you have a significant harvest.

What to Plant

In this garden you'll plant Alpine strawberries, Wild blueberries, Blackberries and Raspberries, Grapes
Difficulty level Easy
Hardiness All zones
Sunlight Full sun
Earliest planting date After average last spring frost

Garden Add-ons

Hoop House Cover the garden with a hoop house starting about four weeks before the average first frost date.
Trellis You'll need a trellis to support your grape vines. For instructions on building a simple trellis, see page 64.

MAINTAINING YOUR BERRY GARDEN

• After planting and for the first month, water daily, directly on the soil at the base of the plants, where the roots are, as the plants establish themselves.
• Water the soil deeply two or three times per week in the early morning, as needed. Be careful not to wet the leaves of the plants.
• To extend the growing season, cover the garden with a hoop house starting about four weeks before the average first frost date. Remove the plastic cover on the hoop house four weeks after your average first frost date and leave it off until the spring. In the spring, four weeks before your average spring frost date, put the plastic back on the hoop house over the garden to jump-start your berry factory and provide fruit earlier.

PLANTS YOU NEED

Strawberries
seed or seedling
1 per 1 sq. ft.

Blueberries
seedling
1 per 2 sq. ft.

Blackberries
seedling
1 per 2 sq. ft.

Raspberries
seedling
1 per 2 sq. ft.

Grapes
seedling
1 per 2 sq. ft.

CONTAINER & RAISED-BED GARDEN PLANS

Container Garden Plan

To grow berry plants in a container you're going to need a large one. Some of these can be pricy, but an inexpensive and sustainable option is a recycled oak barrel, previously used to store wine or spirits. Cut in half, these long-lasting, watertight wooden barrels make great containers for shrubs, vegetables, and flowers. Most large garden centers and nurseries carry these handy, great-looking containers.

PREPARING THE CONTAINER

1. Position the barrel at the spot where it will be permanently located (it will become heavy once it's filled with potting soil and plants).

2. Drill 10 to 20 ¼-inch holes through the bottom of the oak barrel.

3. Add a 1-inch-thick layer of filler—a few handfuls of small stones, pebbles, or gravel—to the bottom of the barrel for proper drainage.

4. Fill the container with organic potting soil and plant according to the instructions; water thoroughly after planting.

:::

WHAT YOU NEED

- ½ oak barrel
- Gravel or filler for proper drainage
- Organic potting soil
- Berry plants

What to Plant in Your Berry Garden

Container A

4 alpine strawberry plants, 2 blueberry plants, 1 blackberry or 1 raspberry plant

Container B

1 grapevine, 2 blackberry or 2 raspberry plants

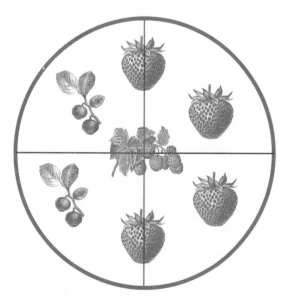

Container Garden Plan A

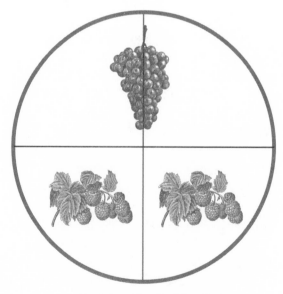

Container Garden Plan B

MAINTAINING THE CONTAINER GARDEN

Containers can dry out quickly, so you'll need to water the soil deeply and often. If the surface is dry, use the finger test to see if the container is still moist 2 inches below the surface. If it is dry, it's time to water thoroughly. Water the surface of the soil until the water runs out of the bottom of the container, do not water the leaves.

Raised Bed Garden Plans

I've packed the most popular berries as well as grapes into this cuisine garden. Don't feel obligated to grow everything I've suggested here; if you like, increase the number of those plants that are your family's favorites.

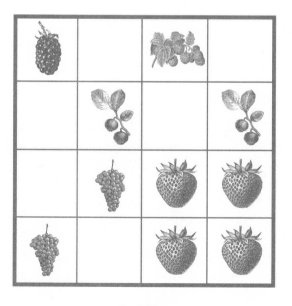

4 x 4 Plan

4 x 8 Plan

STRAWBERRIES

There are two varieties of strawberry plants, ever-bearing and June-bearing. Ever-bearing strawberries bear fruit starting in the spring and don't stop all summer; in some cases, they continue until early winter. Dime-size, the fruit from ever-bearing plants is much smaller than the strawberries you're used to buying at the grocery store. The much larger June-bearing strawberries, which bear fruit only in June, are like the ones available at the grocery store.

The ever-bearing berries you'll be planting in your container garden—alpine strawberries (also known as *fraises des bois*)—have been cultivated for centuries in France as well as in the United States.

The strawberry is a mounding plant, and can grow both horizontally and vertically—as high as 12–18 inches tall—making strawberries perfect for a raised-bed gardens and containers. I love planting alpine strawberries in my garden. Not only are they delicious, they also have beautiful, rich green foliage with pretty white flowers. Red, yellow, and even white alpine strawberries are available.

Strawberries are a great healthy snack, full of vitamin C and iron. They have been used to treat anemia and improve circulation, and they contain pectin, which has been known to lower cholesterol. Strawberries are also an anti-inflammatory—and a gorgeous fruit that's easy to grow, fun to pick, and sweet to eat.

Seed to table 1 year
Transplants to table 6 weeks from planting
Spacing for seeds and transplants 1 per square foot
Native to Alpine mountain region of Italy

STARTING ALPINE STRAWBERRIES FROM SEED

It's cost effective to start alpine strawberries from seed (I've had a lot of success with them), but the plants won't produce fruit the first year. You can order seeds online from e-retailers, such as The Strawberry Store (www.thestrawberrystore.com), which offer a large variety of seeds and lots of information on growing alpine strawberries from seed. Alpines can be difficult to find at garden centers, so order seeds early before they are sold out in the spring.

Once you get the seeds, place them in the freezer in a water-tight container for three or four weeks. When you take them out of the freezer, be prepared to start the seeds indoors with a heat mat and a grow light (see "Make Your Own Hothouse" on page 42). Alpines germinate when the temperature is between 60 and 70 degrees. Keep them moist and be patient. They will start sprouting in about a week, but it may take up to 30 days for about 60 percent of the sown strawberry seeds to germinate.

Because of that relatively low germination rate, start all of your seeds and don't store any. Every year of storage will reduce the germination rate of the seeds. Once your seedlings have at least three leaves, transplant them into a larger container. When the plants are 3–4 inches tall, start hardening them before planting them in the garden (for information about hardening, see page 44).

TRANSPLANTING ALPINE STRAWBERRIES

When you transplant strawberry plants that you've started from seed, all their energy the first year will go into becoming established plants; they won't produce flowers. Transplants sold at the nursery or garden center have already been growing for a year, so you'll be able to start harvesting berries about 6 weeks after planting them in your garden.

The plants are disease resistant and very cold-hardy; once established, they'll remain green through the winter, even after they stop flowering. Pop a hoop house over the plants in early spring as they come back to life so that they'll fill out, bloom early, and set fruit.

Alpines love full sun but prefer partial shade in hot climates. During times of high temperatures—in the 90s to 100 degrees—the blooms may dry out, even if you've watered them well. Don't worry, alpine strawberries are resilient plants and will rebound in no time.

Patti's Picks

Ruegen Improved Alpine Strawberries (*Fragaria vesca*) This popular red alpine variety is hardy and grows up to 18 inches tall.

Baron Solemacher Alpine Strawberries (*Fragaria vesca*) Both the red and white varieties of this strawberry are easy to start from seed. The red variety is sweeter than the white.

Yellow Wonder Alpine Strawberries (*Fragaria vesca*) This highly aromatic, tasty variety is safe from birds—for some reason they don't bother with the berries, which start off white and turn yellow when they're ripe.
Height 12–18 inches; **spread** 18 inches

HARVESTING STRAWBERRIES

Alpine strawberry plants are ever-bearing, which means they produce fruit throughout the growing season, not just once a year like June-bearing strawberries. If you've started your own strawberry plants from seed and planted the seedlings in your raised-bed garden, you won't see any fruit the first year. Alpine strawberry plants purchased from a nursery, especially ones that are already flowering, should begin giving you fruit the first year. You can begin harvesting fruit from mid- to late spring through the first frost. You can also extend the harvest into mid-winter by using a hoop house after the first frost.

If you give a berry a tug and it doesn't pop off, it's not quite ripe. When you're not eating these delicious berries as quickly as you pick them, you can freeze the strawberries for later use or make preserves.

BLUEBERRIES

My mouth waters just thinking about all the delicious things you can make with blueberries—and they're all good for you, too. High in fiber, blueberries are the perfect fruit to help keep your cholesterol low.

Wild blueberries are smaller by nature than cultivated, store-bought blueberries, but they have more antioxidants and more intense flavor, and they're great for freezing, preserving, and baking. The most popular blueberry plant varieties are highbush Jersey and Patriot blueberries, which can grow up to 10 feet and higher in optimum conditions, making them too tall to be planted in raised beds. Highbush varieties are great for planting in your landscape and are good substitutes for a tall hedge. If you want blueberry plants that don't grow much higher than 3 feet, look for more compact varieties.

GROWING BLUEBERRIES

Hardiness zones 3–7 are the best climates for growing blueberries; case in point: the state of Maine is the number-one producer of commercial blueberries in the United States (the lowbush blueberry is the state fruit of Maine).

Although you can plant blueberry bushes in the spring, they're also excellent to plant in the fall, when they're usually on sale. Plant different lowbush or compact varieties so they can cross-pollinate to produce a better-tasting fruit. Plant your blueberry bushes in freshly turned soil. Dig a hole at least the size of the container your blueberry bush is planted in. Water the blueberry bush thoroughly before taking it out of the container, then knock off some of the soil from the root ball and loosen the roots. It's OK if you break off some of the roots while you're transplanting the shrub—in fact, it's good for the plant. Put the plant into the soil, and mulch and water it well.

Keep the plant well watered for a few weeks after planting so the roots can establish themselves. Clip dead or diseased branches, stems, and stalks at any time, but do not prune live branches until you've exhausted your blueberry crop for the year. Allow the berries to ripen before harvesting them. Pick ripe dark blueberries in mid-summer. Once your plants have been established for a few years, you'll get a decent blueberry crop.

Spacing for transplants 1 plant per 2 square feet
Native to North America

Patti's Pick

Northcountry Blueberry (*Vaccinium angustifolium*) Although these plants are self-pollinating, they yield larger crops if they're grown alongside and are pollinated by Northblue blueberries (*Vaccinium angustifolium* 'Northblue'). Northcountry is one of the most adapt-able and prolific varieties. Mature plants yield up to seven pounds of fruit. The compact bushes are great for containers and raised beds, and the dark green summer foliage turns red in the fall.

Height 1½ –2½ feet
Native to North America

HARVESTING BLUEBERRIES

Beginning one year after planting, you will harvest medium-size dark purple berries in mid- to late summer. Allow the berries to ripen on the plant from green to purple to dark purple. You can tell if the ber-ries are ripe if they can easily be plucked off the shrub (it doesn't hurt to taste a few to be sure they're perfectly ripe). These are the sweetest berries and should be eaten within a day or two.

BLACKBERRIES & RASPBERRIES

Blackberries and raspberries are native to the United States and can grow with little maintenance or water. They are also perennials, so they'll provide increasing amounts fruit as the years progress.

Blackberry and raspberry plants grow long canes that flower and produce fruit. In fact, they can produce multiple harvests throughout the growing season because they are biennial. This means that the canes only grow for two years and then die.

New canes, known as primocanes, will grow every year and bear fruit in the fall through the first frost. The next year, these same canes, now called floricanes, will bear fruit in late spring to early summer, and then die. To protect this staggered harvest, prune only diseased or dead, grayish-looking canes that bore fruit in the last year. In late winter, top-dress (fertilize) the plants by mulching around the plants with compost. This will insulate the plants from wintertime cold and give them a boost of food in early spring.

GROWING BLACKBERRIES & RASPBERRIES

There are lots of varieties of blackberries and raspberries to choose from. Your local nurseries and garden centers will carry the varieties that grow well in your area. Buy plants in small containers from the nursery (they're also less expensive than plants purchased in 1-gallon containers or larger) and allow them to become established in your garden for an entire growing season. All of the plants in this bed are planted once and grow year after year, providing a greater harvest with each passing season.

1. Plant blackberries and raspberries in fertile, well-drained soil.

2. Water the plants for the first month to help get them established. The soil should be moist but not wet.

3. During times of drought, water as deeply as needed.

4. Blackberry and raspberry plants tolerate some shade, but they thrive and yield more fruit in sunny areas, especially in cooler climates.

5. Since they can grow as tall as 6 feet, these plants may need a vertical support like a trellis.

PRUNING & PROPAGATING TIPS

• "Tip prune" new canes in the spring. This encourages branching and the growth of thicker canes to support bigger, juicier berries.

• Once new canes reach about 24 inches, cut 6–12 inches off the tip.

• Tip-pruning will delay fruiting significantly, so don't tip-prune all of your new canes and do not prune if flowers have formed on the tip.

• Every spring, new cane shoots will start growing just about everywhere in the bed, including areas where you've put in other plants. Remove rogue shoots regularly so they don't crowd out the other plants in your raised bed. Start another bed if you have room, let new shoots grow in a container on the patio, or plant them right into your landscape. You can also share the wealth with friends and neighbors.

Patti's Picks

Nova Raspberry (*Rubus strigosus*) This sweet, thornless, cold-hardy raspberry cultivated in Nova Scotia tastes just like a raspberry should.
Hardiness Zones 3–8
Height 4–5 feet
Spacing for transplants 1 plant per 2 square feet

Fall Gold Yellow Raspberry (*Rubus idaeus*) Sweet and juicy, this golden variety is great for eating fresh and for canning and preserving.
Hardiness Zones 3–9
Height 3–5 feet

Apache Thornless Blackberry (*Rubus fruticosus*) This jumbo, high-yielding, disease-resistant berry also delivers huge flavor.
Hardiness Zones 5–9
Height 3–6 feet

Triple-Crown Thornless Blackberry (*Rubus fruticosus*) Productivity, flavor, and hardiness are this prolific variety's triple crown. A late-summer ripener, it yields firm and glossy fruit.
Hardiness Zones 5–9
Height 3–5 feet

HARVESTING RASPBERRIES & BLACKBERRIES

In colder climates (zone 7 or colder), you'll have edible raspberries and blackberries throughout the spring, summer, and fall, starting one year after planting. In warmer climates (zones 8–10) you'll have a great harvest in late summer and early fall.

GRAPES

If you're surprised to see grapes in a "berry" garden, you're not alone. Many people don't think of grapes as berries, but in fact they are. Grapes are wonderfully companionable with berries, as you'll see in my recipe for Grape-Berry Juice on page 182, and the leaves provide the perfect wrap for a delicious savory filling (see page 186 for my Dolmades recipe). And what could be more pleasant than a shady grape arbor in your summer garden?

Homegrown grapes are such a treat to eat, and they are incredibly versatile as a fruity, late-summer snack eaten straight off the vine, as juice, or as jelly, jam, or even raisins. It takes a few years, however, before grape plants begin to produce, and up to five years before you get a good harvest, but they are worth the wait.

Grapes are low in calories, high in vitamin C, and have regenerative properties that work on the cellular level. Feel free to add them to your diet and reap the health benefits.

Grapes are thought to be one of the oldest cultivated fruits, going back thousands of years to the world's oldest human cultures. Grapes from southern Europe are known as Old World grapes, but various species of New World grapes grew in the wild and were a part of the diet of many Native Americans. Concord grapes, one of the most popular grapes cultivated and eaten in America today (and a favorite for making grape jelly) are actually a cross between an Old World grape variety that doesn't winter well and a New World variety that is cold-hardy.

GROWING GRAPES

When you choose grapes to plant in your garden, consider planting just one variety— there's no need to have multiple varieties, especially if you have a small garden. Some grapes are self-pollinating, so you can have grapes even if you have only a single vine. For example, some varieties of muscadines (a Native American grape), do not require another plant for cross-pollination and produce grapes that can be eaten straight off the vine or made into wine, jam, or preserves. If you choose to plant multiple varieties, plant disease-resistant grapes that ripen at different times for a staggered harvest.

Since grapevines can become very large plants, they need a structure that will provide vertical support, like a trellis. (You can purchase a grapevine trellis or make one yourself. Very little construction is required, and the materials are simple to find. For information about building a trellis see page 64.

In the first year of the growth of a grapevine, all you'll see is a big, beautiful vine, which can grow up to 20 feet per year. To support the vine and get the most out of it, don't attach it to the trellis going straight up. Instead, train the vine to grow horizontally. Over time, new branches will grow vertically. In the second year, starting in early spring, prune your grapevines so that each cane or branch has about five buds. Every year afterward, cut the canes back and continue increasing the number of buds on the cane. Fertilize with a top dressing of compost.

Spacing for transplanted vines 1 per 2 square feet

Patti's Picks

Sweet Lace Grapes (*Vitis vinifera*) This delicious table and wine grape is one of my favorites; it grows well in raised beds and is perfect as a patio container plant. The intricate lace pattern of the leaves also provides an elegant texture in the garden. Harvest in late summer.
Hardiness Zones 6–9
Native to France

Concord Grapes (*Vitis labrusca*) This is the classic American variety used to make grape juice and jelly, but the grapes taste even better fresh. Harvest in early fall.
Hardiness Zones 5–9
Native to North America

HARVESTING GRAPES

As temperatures warm up, you'll see tiny bunches of flowers growing on the vines, and very quickly they'll start forming into grapes. The tiny grapes will start off green and change color when they're ripe, depending on the variety.

When you smell a strong sweet grape scent around your vines, you'll know that it's time to harvest the grapes. The best way to pick the right bunch is to taste a grape and see if it is slightly squishy and sweet. If it is hard and tart the grapes need more time on the vine.

HONEY SIMPLE SYRUP

Makes 2 cups

This simple syrup is great for sweetening juices, hot or cold teas, lemonade, or drizzled on a fruit salad.

1 cup raw organic honey or Golden Blossom honey

1 cup water

1 cup mint or lemon balm leaves

Bring ingredients to a boil in a medium saucepan until all the honey is dissolved. Let the syrup sit for 30 minutes to one hour, strain, and store in a glass jar. You can keep the syrup in the fridge for up to two weeks.

BERRY RECIPES

Grape-Berry Juice

Makes four 8-oz. servings

Over time, your grape harvest will increase. Grapes have antibacterial properties, so making grape juice is a healthy way to drink them up.

2	lbs. grapes
16	oz. blueberries, raspberries, strawberries, or blackberries, fresh or frozen
1	cup honey simple syrup (see recipe, left) or raw agave nectar, to taste
16	oz. water
1	tray ice cubes
4	12-inch sprigs mint or lemon balm

Juice or puree the grapes until you have 16 ounces of grape juice; place it in the refrigerator. Puree 8 ounces, or half, of the berries. Coarsely chop the remaining berries. Combine the grape juice with the pureed berries in a large pitcher and stir with a spoon. Add the remaining berries and stir. Sweeten with honey simple syrup or raw agave nectar to taste. Dilute with water to taste. Chill pitcher in fridge. Serve juice with ice and a sprig of mint as garnish. The juice will last in the fridge for about 5 days.

Mixed Berry Salad

Serves four to six

This colorful salad is great for casual meals and picnics, or dress it up with a scoop of vanilla or coconut milk ice cream for a special dessert.

1	lb. seasonal berries (any mix)
2	tbsp. minced mint leaves
	Honey simple syrup, to taste
	Juice of 1 lemon or lime

Mix ingredients in a large bowl. Cover and chill for at least an hour and serve with an extra drizzle of honey simple syrup.

Seriously Simple Jam

Makes one 16-ounce jar

If you like your jam sweet and chunky, try this fast and easy "no cook" recipe.

1   lb. berries (any mixture)

1   cup or more organic turbinado raw sugar

In a large bowl, mash berries, adding sugar to taste until the sugar is completely dissolved. The jam lasts for about a week stored in a glass jar in the fridge and can be used as a topping on waffles, pancakes, French toast, muffins, or scones.

Berry Preserves

Makes 16 ounces

This quick recipe is an easy way to preserve your berry harvest.

1   lb. fresh berries

1   cup organic turbinado raw sugar

¼   cup water

½   lemon, thinly sliced

    Juice of ½ lemon

Put all ingredients in a large saucepan and simmer until thick, about 20 minutes. Cool and store the jam in a covered jar. It will stay fresh for up to two weeks in the fridge.

**HOW TO
VACUUM-SEAL
MASON JARS**

Tightly cover each jar
of warm, newly cooked
jam with its lid.
Place the jars in a large
pot and fill with enough
water to cover the jars by
about 2 inches. Bring the
water to a boil and leave
the jars in the boiling
water for 20 minutes.
Using tongs, carefully
remove the jars and
allow them to cool on a
dishtowel on the kitchen
counter. Cooling the jars
to room temperature will
complete the vacuum-
sealing process.

Grape Blueberry Jelly

Makes three 16-ounce jars

My family—particularly my husband, who likes the bits of blueberry in this jelly—begs me to make this recipe every year. There is no need to add sugar; the intense sweetness of the grapes and blueberries—and the addition of pectin in this jelly takes it over the top.

5 lbs. Concord grapes

2 lbs. blueberries

1 packet Ball® RealFruit™ No-Sugar Pectin

Put grapes through a food mill to extract about 5 or 6 cups of juice and set aside. Then put half the blueberries through the food mill and put the juice aside. Put the other half of the blueberries in a large bowl, add the grape and blueberry juice, and stir. If you don't want chunks of blueberry fruit in the jelly, process all the blueberries through the food mill. Place the grape and blueberry juice mixture in a large saucepan and mix in the package of pectin. Bring to a full boil, stirring frequently for about 2 minutes, then reduce the heat to a simmer. To test the consistency, scoop up a spoonful of jelly with an ice-cold spoon. Allow the jelly to cool on the spoon. If it's not thick enough for your taste, keep it simmering on the stove for 1 or 2 more minutes and repeat the test. Once the jelly has thickened to your liking, turn off the stove and let it cool for 5 minutes, then give it a mix, and ladle it into sterilized glass Mason jars, leaving 1 inch of space at the top of the jar. Vacuum-seal the jars according to the instructions given at left, so that they can be safely stored in your pantry without spoiling. Store open jars in the refrigerator.

Raspberry & Herb Vinaigrette

Makes about 1 cup

Once you've mastered this recipe, always make an extra batch to store in the fridge, then pour it on so many different dishes. It is the perfect dressing for a fresh salad of spinach leaves, crumbled goat cheese, alpine strawberries, and crushed walnuts.

For the Aioli Garlic Mustard

1	garlic clove
¼	tsp. coarse kosher salt
1	cup prepared mayonnaise (store-bought is fine)
2	tbsp. Dijon mustard
1	tbsp. fresh lemon juice
	Pepper, fresh ground, to taste

In a small bowl mash garlic and salt into a paste. Mix in the remaining ingredients and blend thoroughly. Season to taste with pepper and additional salt, if desired.

For the vinaigrette

½	cup raspberries, fresh or frozen
¼	cup apple cider vinegar
¼	cup balsamic vinegar
2	tsp. raw sugar
1	tbsp. aioli garlic mustard
½	cup olive oil
10	mint or basil leaves
	Pinch of ground white pepper
	Juice of ½ lemon
1	tsp. minced shallots
½	cup olive oil

Add all ingredients, except oil, to a blender or food processor and puree until smooth. Slowly add oil to mixture in blender or food processor and pulse until combined well. Store in a glass jar in the fridge for up to two weeks.

Dolmades (Stuffed Grape Leaves)

Makes 30-40 dolmades

Grapevines grow lots and lots of leaves. Luckily, they can be used to make a truly special treat. The lamb and spices in this recipe make a filling appetizer, but you can also swap in a combination of vegetables or take things to a sweeter level and stuff the grape leaves with nuts and fruit.

¼	cup olive oil (for coating the sauté pan)
½	cup chopped green onions (scallions)
½	cup cubed tomatoes
1	lb. ground lamb
½	cup rice
	zest of 1 lemon
¼	cup coarsely chopped pine nuts
3	tbsp. allspice
	Salt and pepper, to taste
½	cup chopped fresh parsley
½	cup fresh mint
½	cup fresh dill
½	cup raisins or chopped dried figs
30–40	medium-size grape leaves
	Juice of 1 lemon
2	cups water

TO MAKE THE FILLING

In a large, heavy-based pan, sauté scallions in oil for 5 minutes or until soft over medium heat, then add cubed tomatoes. Mix and cook for 2 minutes, then add lamb, rice, lemon zest, pine nuts, allspice, and salt and pepper. Sauté until the lamb is cooked, then add 1 cup of water. Mix and simmer until the liquid is absorbed and rice is al dente, about 10 minutes. Take the pan off the stove and mix in the fresh herbs and raisins (or chopped dried figs). Allow the stuffing to cool in a bowl.

STUFFING THE GRAPE LEAVES

While the stuffing is cooling, in a large pot, blanch medium-size grape leaves in simmering water for 5 minutes, then drain the leaves. Pour cold water over the leaves to stop the cooking process. Pat each leaf dry with paper towels and set aside. Lay out the grape leaves underside up, one by one, on a flat surface and put 1 or 2 teaspoons of filling in the center of each grape leaf. Fold the stem end of grape leaf over the filling. Fold the sides over the middle, then roll the stuffed leaf into a cigar shape. Place each stuffed grape leaf in a large deep skillet seam side down. Repeat the process until you have one layer of dolmades in the skillet.

COOKING THE DOLMADES

Pour water and lemon juice over the dolmades so that the rolls are covered halfway with the liquid. Cover the pan and bring to a simmer on the stove over medium heat until the water has evaporated, about 30 minutes or more. The dolmades will be ready when you can easily pierce them with a fork. Meat dolmades should be eaten warm. Vegetarian or sweet dolmades can be served either hot or cold. Dolmades go well with tomato sauce on the side or, more traditionally, with Greek yogurt.

CHAPTER TWELVE

THREE SISTERS NATIVE AMERICAN GARDEN

When Europeans began exploring North America, they saw fields of crops they had never seen before. Among them were corn, beans, squash, sunflowers, and many other foods that we still eat. In fact, three out of four foods consumed around the world today were first cultivated by natives of the Americas. We have much to learn from their ancient agricultural practices.

Today's big agri-farms practice *monocropping*—using chemical fertilizers, they plant a single crop year after year on the same land. Native Americans practiced *polyculture,* planting multiple food crops, along with flowers and cotton, in the same field. In the Mayan *milpa* system, more than 200 different crops were grown on what were bascially vast garden plots.

North American natives also practiced *companion planting*—cultivating crops that grow well together, such as corn, beans, and squash. Because of their reliability as sustaining crops, that trio became known as the Three Sisters. Each supports the other. Through a process called nitrogen fixation, pole beans and other legumes convert nitrogen in the soil into a form that plants such as corn use as they grow. Corn stalks provide a natural trellis for beans to climb and grow on; that structure gives the stalks enough rigidity to withstand high winds and heavy rains. Squash, the third "sister," shades the soil with its long vines and large leaves, keeping it cool and moist and preventing unwanted seeds in the soil from germinating.

The twist in this cuisine garden is edible flowers, which were also grown by Native Americans. A great companion plant, the nasturtium helps ward off garden pests, too. Sunflowers brighten up a garden, and their seeds are a nutritious snack. Native Americans figured this all out for us. Let's give it a try.

GROWING THE THREE SISTERS GARDEN

The plants in this garden can be started from seed in a raised bed, but gardeners in areas with shorter growing seasons should start their corn and squash indoors as both require warm soil temperatures to germinate outside. The seed-starting kit I use (you can buy Native American seeds at www.nativeseeds.org) comes with a light and a heating pad so that the seeds can germinate in time to be planted outside.

1. Plant corn, sunflowers, and nasturtium seeds in your garden starting two weeks after the last frost. Sow seeds 1½ inches deep or use transplants.

2. Cover the garden bed with a hoop house until seeds have germinated or plants are well established.

3. Once the plants are 4 inches tall, water, weed, and mulch around the plants, and water them again. Then plant the beans and squash from seed. Keep the newly sown area moist until the seeds germinate. You can also plant bean and squash seedlings at this time.

4. Water and weed the garden regularly, allowing the soil to dry between waterings.

5. You'll be able to harvest some corn within 70 days, depending on the variety. Sunflowers will be in bloom starting 70 days after planting.

What to Plant

In this garden you'll plant Corn, Sunflowers, Nasturtiums, Beans, and Squash.
Difficulty level Intermediate
Zones All
Sunlight Full sun
Earliest planting date Two weeks after the average last spring frost

Garden Add-ons

Hoop House If you live in zones 3–8, protect your garden with a hoop house until average nighttime temperatures are in the 50s.

PLANTS YOU NEED

Corn
seed or seedling
4 per 1 sq. ft.

Sunflowers
seed or seedling
4 per 1 sq. ft.

Nasturtiums
seed or seedling
1 at each corner
of a raised bed
and at 1-ft.
intervals around
its perimeter

Beans
seed or seedling
5 per 1 sq. ft.

Squash
seed or seedling
1 per 4 sq. ft.

CONTAINER & RAISED-BED GARDEN PLANS

....

WHAT YOU NEED

....

- A large container, at least 24 in. in diameter, with drainage holes
- Gravel or filler for proper drainage
- Organic potting soil
- Seeds
- Watering can
- Plant markers and tags

Container Garden

Yes, a Three Sisters garden can be grown in a container . . . well, sort of. While there are quite a few varieties of corn, beans, nasturtiums, and sunflowers that grow really well in containers, there's just not enough room for squash in this one. Be sure to use a large container that has a minimum diameter of 24 inches so that you can grow a lot of plants in it.

PLANTING THE CONTAINER FROM SEED

1. Add a 2-inch-thick layer of gravel or filler in the bottom of the container, then fill it with potting soil up to 2 inches from the top of the container.

2. Water thoroughly.

3. Plant 1 sunflower seed 1 inch deep in the center of the container, then plant 4 corn seeds around it—about 6 inches away from the sunflower seed.

4. It's also time to plant the nasturtiums: Plant a total of 4 nasturtium seeds around the perimeter of the container, leaving space between each one for the bean seeds (see step 7).

5. Water with a watering can.

6. Keep the soil moist until the seeds germinate. Then allow the soil to dry between waterings.

7. Once the corn is at least 4 inches tall, water the container and plant 8 bean seeds around the perimeter of the container (6 inches away from the corn). Water with a watering can.

8. Keep the container moist until the bean and nasturtium seeds have germinated. Then water regularly, allowing the soil to dry between waterings.

Raised-Bed Garden Plans

Raised beds are the best way to get the most out of your Three Sisters garden, in which each plant has an important role to play. Giving them each the space they need to thrive will help the entire garden reach its full potential.

Whether you choose the 4 x 4 or the 4 x 8 plan, it's important to pay attention to the arrangement of the plants so that they can all help each other grow. Clumping all your corn or beans at one end would defeat the purpose. It's all about balance.

In both the A versions of the Three Sisters garden plan shown here and the B versions on page 192, nasturtiums are planted at 1-ft. intervals around the perimeter of the beds. Squash are planted in the center of each 4' x 4' bed or half bed, amid corn, beans, and sunflowers.

4 x 4 Plan A

4 x 8 Plan A

Once you get the hang of spacing your seeds, perhaps in your second growing season, you can try more creative spacing arrangements, as in the plans shown here. Remember that even in a Three Sisters Native American garden, with its multiple, mutually supportive crops, crop rotation is important for keeping soil healthy, so feel free to rearrange the plants from bed to bed and from year to year.

In all of the Three Sisters garden plans, the beans are planted next to corn for structural support as they grow. The squash is in the middle for shade, and the nasturtiums form a protective barrier around the border to ward off garden pests.

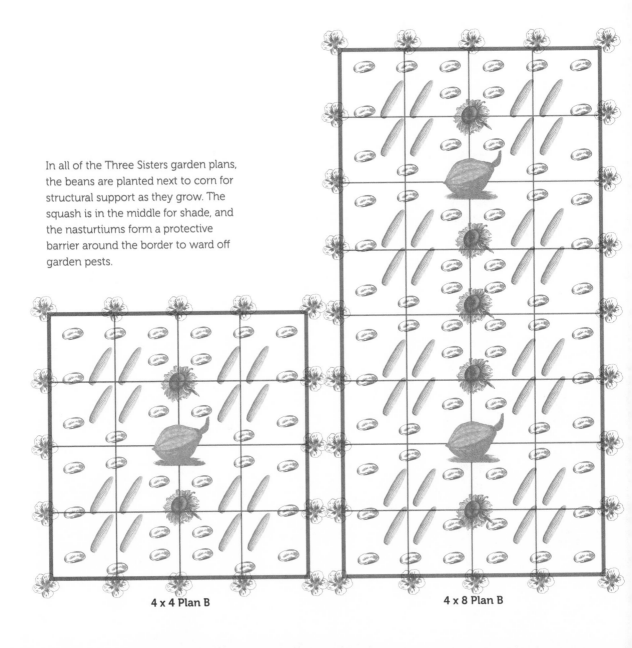

4 x 4 Plan B

4 x 8 Plan B

CORN

Maize is the name Central and South Americans use for corn, which was originally cultivated in Mesoamerica from a wild grass called *teosinte*. In those early days, cultivation produced very small corncobs with few kernels, but over the millennia the cobs evolved and grew bigger and bigger. As early generations of corn traveled to other nations, such as the Aztecs and the Incas, a new diverse breed of edible maize fed millions of people. In fact, 80 percent of the Mayan diet consisted of corn—making it a truly important crop in the history of the Americas.

The corn sold at the grocery store today is a far cry from the traditional varieties that were originally cultivated and that ranged in color from yellow to orange, and from red to blue—sometimes all on the same ear. Native Americans have made painstaking efforts to preserve and grow these varieties, which are a huge part of their heritage. In my garden, I grow many types of corn, including Native American varieties and newer hybrids.

One stalk of traditional corn can produce multiple ears, unlike newer hybrids and genetically modified corn, which are bred to grow only one ear so that it can be easily machine-harvested. The United States is the largest producer of corn in the world. Much of the U.S. crop is used as feed for livestock and to produce ethanol.

Corn has a lot of starch, which means it's high in sugar, especially when it is processed into high-fructose corn syrup—a product that is used in many foods and that has been demonized for contributing to weight gain and high levels of obesity in the United States. However, if you eat corn in moderation, when it's in season, it's a good source of antioxidants, fiber, and vitamins.

You can start planting corn seeds right in your garden two weeks after the average last spring frost. Water the soil, then plant four seeds per square foot, 1½ inches into the soil, and water again with a watering can. Keep the soil moist, and within seven to ten days your seeds will germinate. You may have heard about mounding soil and planting corn seeds in mounds. This is a Native American technique, but since we're using raised beds we don't need to mound the soil.

Spacing for seeds and transplants 4 per square foot

Seed to table 70–100 days

Native to Central and South America

Patti's Picks

Dakota Black Popcorn (Zea mays) This is a great cool-weather variety popular with the Dakota nation. This one is a personal favorite because it's ideal for the climate in my area and delicious eaten fresh or grilled. The 8-inch ears are purple-black.

Golden Bantam Improved (Zea mays) This is the ultimate sweet corn; the ears grow up to 12 inches and are ideal for grilling.
Height The two varieties above (tall corn) grow to up to 12 feet tall.

Hopi Blue Corn (Zea mays) When eaten raw this blue corn has a wonderfully meaty quality. The Hopi let it dry on the stalk and use it to make flour for blue tortillas, and so can you (see page 202). The beautiful purple-blue kernels grow on 9-inch ears.

Hopi Sweet Corn (Zea mays) This yellow variety grows taller than Hopi Blue. It's the perfect, traditional sweet corn—delicious eaten fresh or in cornbread. Bright yellow kernels grow on 9-inch ears.
Height The two varieties above (medium-tall corn) grow to between 5 and 7 feet tall.

Blue Jade Corn (Zea mays) This shorter stalk produces multiple 8-inch ears of blue corn.
Height Around 3 feet

Strawberry Popcorn (Zea mays) Multiple cobs with red kernels grow 2–3 inches long. Allow the cobs to dry on the stalk and use them ornamentally, or take the dried red kernels off the cob and enjoy a unique popcorn on movie night.
Height 4 feet

PESTS & DISEASES

Diseases aren't much of a problem for corn, and insects can easily be controlled. Birds and other critters can also be kept away with little effort. Your plants will stay healthy— and they'll withstand some nibbling from insects—if you plant your corn in well-drained soil that has the right balance of nutrients. To keep future crops disease-free, compost old cornstalks or discard them. This will keep insects and diseases from "overwintering" and coming back the next season to prey on your new plants.

HARVESTING CORN

Harvest corn when the silk on each ear has turned brown. To check if your corn is ripe, peel a bit of the husk off an ear and check the cob to see if the kernels are plump. Pop off a kernel and squeeze it to see if the juice is milky. If it is, you're good to go. Try tasting it too. Sometimes my corn doesn't make it to the kitchen. It's delicious freshly picked and eaten raw.

SAVING SEEDS

To save corn seeds, let some of the ears in your garden dry out completely, right on the stalk. Make sure you pick the corn before the first frost. Pop the kernels off the cob, place them in a paper bag, and allow them to dry out a little bit longer in a cool dark place. Once they are completely dry, store the kernels in glass jars in a cool place until spring.

SUNFLOWERS

Sunflowers come in a variety of colors and sizes. Native Americans used the seeds as snacks and ate sunflower seed cakes and breads, just as we do today. The Hopi used parts of the sunflower to make vivid red, purple, and blue dyes. Every time I see sunflowers in my garden they instantly put a big smile on my face.

There are three different categories of sunflowers: giant, regular, and mini. For the raised beds in our Three Sisters Native American garden, however, we're going to stick with regular and mini varieties. The best way to plant sunflowers is to start them from seed right in the garden. Before planting, water the soil, then plant the sunflower seeds, 4 per square foot and at least 1 inch deep. Water the area again with a watering can after planting. Keep the soil moist until the seeds germinate.

Sunflowers are so much fun and so easy to grow that I usually plant extras right in the garden and transplant them elsewhere once they are at least 4 inches high.

Spacing for seeds and transplants 4 per square foot
From seed to bloom 70 days
Native to North America

Patti's Picks

Arikara Sunflower (*Helianthus annuus*) This native sunflower grows multiple heads with edible seeds.

Apache Brown Striped Sunflower (*Helianthus annuus*) Popular with the Apache nation, this sunflower yields black- or brown- and white-striped sunflower seeds.

Hopi Black Dye Sunflower (*Helianthus annuus*) This traditional sunflower has large heads and abundant, edible black-shelled seeds. The Hopis used the seeds for making dye.

Height These large sunflowers grow very tall—up to 12 feet tall.

PESTS & DISEASES

You will encounter some garden pests when you grow sunflowers, but there's not too much you can do about that. Keeping your bird feeders well stocked throughout the growing season can help keep birds away from your sunflowers and other tempting treats that grow in your garden.

HARVESTING SUNFLOWERS

To harvest sunflowers for the seeds, cut the flower head off the stem. You can tell if the seeds are ready to be harvested if the back of the flower head is dry and brown. Do not harvest after a rain, and make sure the flower head is quite dry. Just rub or brush the plump seeds out of the head by hand. Dry the seeds and store them in a glass jar, shell and all, for later use. You can eat the sunflower seeds raw or roast them before eating. In the spring you can use them to plant more sunflowers.

NASTURTIUMS

This wonderful annual, which the Incas grew, produces edible flowers and spectacular round leaves. (The delicate flowers have a pleasant peppery flavor.) A great companion plant, nasturtiums make the Three Sisters Native American garden a more balanced ecosystem by helping to ward off pests.

Start the seeds in the garden, right where you want them to grow, starting two weeks after the average last spring frost date. The seeds of this plant are quite large and are not uniform in shape. To make sure the seeds germinate quickly, scar them by scraping them along a rough surface—like concrete or brick. Just a little bit of filing is all that's required; you want to the seed to remain intact. Keep the soil moist until the seeds germinate in seven to ten days. For a while, you'll just see the round leaves growing. Once the plant starts flowering, it will continue to do so until the fall.

Spacing for seeds and transplants 1 per square foot
From seed to bloom 70 days
Native to North America

Patti's Picks

Fiesta Blend (*Tropaeolum majus*) This native annual has yellow peach and bright orange edible flowers.
Height 10–12 inches

Dwarf Nasturtium (*Tropaeolum minus*) This nasturtium has beautiful yellow to orange petals.
Height Vine trails up to 10 feet

PEST & DISEASES

To prevent pests and diseases prune off any yellow or dead leaves and branches throughout the growing season and pop them into your compost bin. Deer and rabbits will stay away from your nasturtiums because they just don't like the taste of these plants.

HARVESTING NASTURTIUMS

Harvest the flowers by cutting off a bit of the stem, along with the flowers, and put the stems in a jar of water. Place the jar in the fridge until you're ready to use the flowers. The leaves are also edible and can be added to a mixed green salad or used as garnish.

SAVING SEEDS

If you want to save nasturtium seeds, don't pick all of your flowers— let some go to seed. You'll see a cluster of green seeds once the flower petals have wilted. You can pick these clusters and dry them out on a tray lined with paper towels. Place the tray in a cool dark place for a few weeks. You can also let the seeds mature on the plant and collect them when they've fallen off the plant— if the birds don't get to them first.

BEANS

Beans are essential to the Three Sisters garden because of their nitrogen-fixating prokaryotes (single-celled organisms on their roots), which convert nitrogen from the air into compounds used by plants. Beans are both delicious and nutritious; they are high in dietary fiber, vitamin C, and iron, important nutrients that help prevent disease. Native Americans ate them throughout the winter; once beans are dried and shelled, they can be stored for long periods. A favorite traditional dish is succotash, a tasty combo of corn, kidney or lima beans, and squash (see the recipe on page 201).

Once your corn is 4 inches tall, it's time to plant beans. (Corn needs the head start because beans grow so quickly they can choke corn and keep it from growing.) Water the soil before you plant bean seeds in your garden. I lay the large seeds on the soil where I want to plant them, then gently push them into the soil, about 1½ inches down. Cover the seeds well.

The seeds will germinate before you know it, so be sure to have a vertical support in place before you plant them. Keep the soil moist until the seeds germinate, and put mulch around the plants when they're about 4 inches tall. As the vines grow they'll twist around the support and will also migrate for support to any cornstalks and sunflowers that are growing nearby.

Seed to table 70 days
Spacing for seeds 5 per square foot
Native to the Americas

Patti's Picks

Blue Lake Pole Beans (*Phaseolus vulgaris* var. *vulgaris*) Great eaten raw or as a side dish, this is the classic American green bean variety.

Tepehuan Red Kidney Bean (*Phaseolus vulgaris*) This is a traditional Native American red kidney bean variety.
Height Vines will grow up to 12 feet long

PESTS & DISEASES
You can protect your green beans by choosing varieties that are resistant to diseases that are common in your area and by purchasing seeds from a reputable seed company. Make sure the soil is adequately

HOW TO
DRY BEANS

Once you've allowed a large number of bean pods to mature and dry in your garden, pull them off, take them inside, and allow them to continue to dry in a cool dark place.

Then remove the dried beans from the pods and store them in glass jars for future use.

You can use the dried beans when making soups by soaking the beans in water (1 cup dried beans to 2½ cups water) for a minimum of 1 hour before cooking. Delicious.

fertilized, and rotate beans with other plants in your garden. Be sure to remove old plants from your raised beds after the harvest so that any diseases or insects that might be present won't have a place to stick around next season. The same advice holds for kidney beans. To help keep insects at bay, plant aromatic herbs nearby, such as rosemary, to deter bean beetles, and nasturtiums, which keep away aphids and white flies.

HARVESTING BEANS

It's time to harvest your beans when you notice little flowers forming on the plants where the pods will eventually grow. It's amazing to see how large the pods can become—up to 12 inches. Pick the pods when they're young and the beans inside haven't quite formed. At this point, you can eat them whole—they're delicious in salads. Pick medium-size pods if you want to prepare the beans in a cooked dish.

SAVING THE SEEDS

If you want to preserve some bean seeds for future use, grow them to maturity and allow the pods to dry. Pick the pods off the plants and remove the beans from the pods. Store them in a glass jar until the next growing season.

SQUASH

Squash is a delicious addition to everyday cooking, but somewhere along the line it lost its popularity in American cuisine. Squash is making a comeback, though, because it is so easy to grow and there are so many ways to prepare it. Many more stores are now carrying it too. It's a great vegetable for a seasonal diet.

Bush varieties can be grown in containers, but our Native American garden calls for squash that grows on vines. Pumpkin and squash are actually the same thing, but in various parts of the world, the terms are used differently. In Australia, for example, the term "pumpkin" is used for all kinds of squashes. In the U.S., we differentiate winter squash, summer squash, and zucchini from pumpkins, but they are the same plants, botanically speaking, despite a lot of variety in shape, color, size, and taste. You can grow and care for them all in the same way, but they have different uses in the kitchen.

It's best to start squash from seed right in the garden because it's easy and economical. Plant the seed 1 inch deep and keep the soil moist until it germinates. As the vine grows, flowers will form, and if bees and other pollinating insects do their job, more than one squash will form per vine.

Seed to table 70 days
Spacing for seeds 1 per 4 square feet
Native to North America

Patti's Picks

Fordhook Acorn Squash (*Cucurbita pepo*) This rare American heirloom squash with a cream- to peach-colored skin has been around for more than 100 years. It ripens early, around the same time as your corn.

Hopi Pumpkin (*Cucurbita maxima*) This vining pumpkin has long been grown by the Hopi nation. A variety of winter squash, Hopi pumpkin is an easy-to-grow, low-maintenance plant. Depending on the variety, these pumpkin-shaped squash can be green or orange when they're ripe.

PESTS & DISEASES

Remove any brown, yellow, or dead leaves to prevent pest and diseases, and allow the surface of the soil to dry between waterings.

HARVESTING SQUASHES & PUMPKINS

Depending on the variety of squash, the color of the skin will tell you when it's time to harvest it. You'll also know when your squash is ready to harvest when the plant itself begins to die. Remove the squash or pumpkin from the vine with a pruning shears at the stem. It will store nicely for a week or more in the kitchen until you're ready to use it.

RECIPES FOR A NATIVE AMERICAN GARDEN

I think you'll enjoy these recipes—they're a little different and will give you a taste of traditional Native American foods that you might not get every day. After you've made a couple of these easy, flavorful recipes, don't be surprised if they make their way into your permanent repertoire.

Three Sisters Succotash

Serves four

Not only do the Three Sisters grow well together, they also taste great when combined in this traditional dish.

½	cup chopped green onions
1	tbsp. olive oil
2	cups cubed squash (any kind)
2	cups green beans
2	cups fresh corn
1	hot pepper, deseeded and minced
2	cups vegetable stock
6	large sage leaves, minced
4	tbsp. unsalted organic butter
	Sea salt and freshly ground pepper, to taste

Sauté green onions in olive oil until soft in large skillet over medium-high heat for 2 minutes or until soft. Add squash, beans, corn, and hot pepper and sauté for about 1 minute. Add vegetable stock and mix. Bring the mixture to a boil and simmer, uncovered, over low heat until the vegetables are cooked and the stock has reduced, around 10 minutes. Stir in the remaining ingredients and add salt and pepper to taste.

Variation You can turn this succotash recipe into a hearty soup by adding 3 more cups of vegetable stock, 1 cup of shelled sunflower seeds, and 1½ cups of diced potatoes. Garnish with nasturtium blossoms and finely chopped sage. Serve with Sunflower Seed Cake (see recipe on page 205).

HOW TO MAKE CORNMEAL

Place dried corn kernels into a grain grinder or mill (available for around $40) and grind at least three times to produce fine corn meal.

Blue Corn Tortillas

Serves four

I love the flavor and aroma of homemade tortillas when I'm rustling them up in my kitchen. These blue corn tortillas are fantastic stuffed with salad greens, meat, cheese, and veggies. You'll love them sprinkled with sugar or drizzled with honey or maple syrup. They're also fun to make with kids—and they taste better than any tortilla you can buy at the store.

2	cups water
1	tbsp. salt
2	cups blue cornmeal
	Vegetable oil for skillet

Boil the water and salt. In a large mixing bowl, add the cornmeal and mix with water, little by little, until a dough is formed. Allow the dough to cool enough so that you can divide it with your hands into 2-inch balls. On a well-floured surface, use a rolling pin to flatten each ball of dough into a thin round tortilla. Brown on both sides in a lightly oiled skillet or griddle over medium heat, about 2 minutes on each side. Keep the tortillas warm in a clean dishtowel until it's time to serve them.

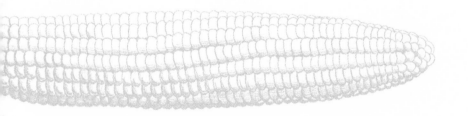

Native American–Style Cornbread

Serves six

Cornbread is great served hot, right out of the oven, as a warm snack. It is also the perfect sop for stew, and just the thing to have with a bowl of soup.

½	cup whole-wheat flour
¾	cup white flour
¾	cup cornmeal
¼	cup sugar
5	tsp. baking powder
½	teaspoon salt
⅓	cup maple syrup or honey
½	cup low fat milk
½	cup water
1	tsp. vanilla extract

Mix all of the dry ingredients together in a large bowl. Mix the wet ingredients in a separate bowl. Add the wet ingredients to the dry ingredients and mix well. Bake at 375°F in a greased 8-inch x 8-inch baking pan for about 30 minutes, or until golden brown. Serve warm with softened butter on the side.

HOW TO DRY CORN

You can harvest fresh corn and dry it using this method:

Boil corncobs in water for 5 minutes. Remove the cobs and cool them in ice water to stop them from cooking.

Remove the cobs from cold water and dry them off.

Place the cobs on cookie sheets in the oven at 150°F for about 8 hours, rotating the cobs regularly so that all of the kernels dry evenly.

Remove the cobs from the oven and store them in a paper bag for a week to ensure they are completely dry.

Pop the kernels off the cobs and store them in glass jars.

You can use dried corn kernels when making soups by soaking the corn in water (1 cup dried corn to 2¼ cups water) for a minimum of a half hour before cooking. Dried corn can also be ground or milled into corn meal and used to make corn bread or tortillas.

Roasted Squash Soup with Ginger

Serves four

Autumn weather and roasted squash soup just go together. As the days get shorter and cooler a warm bowl of this creamy soup hits the spot.

1	butternut or acorn squash (1–2 lbs.), seeded and cut into pieces
3	tbsp. olive oil
4	cloves garlic, minced
2	tsp. minced fresh ginger
1	cup chopped green onions
3	celery stalks, thinly sliced
4	cups vegetable broth
3	tsp. finely chopped sage
½	cup heavy cream
	Salt and pepper, to taste
4–8	nasturtium flowers for garnish

Preheat oven to 400°F. Coat the squash with some of the olive oil, reserving about 2 tablespoons. Place the squash on a baking sheet, cut side up, and sprinkle with a few pinches of sea salt. Roast the squash in the oven until soft, about 40–50 minutes . While the squash is cooling, sauté the garlic, ginger, and green onions in a large soup pot, using the reserved olive oil for 2 minutes or so. Add the celery and sauté for another 2 minutes. Remove the peel from the roasted squash with a paring knife. Add squash to the soup pot and stir. Add the vegetable broth and sage. Bring to a boil, then reduce heat to medium-low. Cover and simmer for 10–15 minutes, stirring often. Let the soup cool for 15 minutes or so, then blend it, using a hand mixer (or puree it in a blender) until the soup is smooth. Add the cream and blend again. Season with salt and pepper to taste. Garnish with nasturtium flowers and serve.

Sunflower Seed Cake

Serves six

It doesn't take any time at all to make these delicious, grain-free cakes. They make a nutritious snack and a satisfying accompaniment to a good bowl of hot soup.

- 3 cups raw, shelled sunflower seeds
- 3 cups water
- 3 tbsp. maple syrup or raw agave nectar
- ½ cup fine organic blue cornmeal
- ½ cup vegetable oil

Simmer the seeds in water for about 1 hour. Drain and grind the seeds into a paste, using a mortar and pestle. Mix the syrup and cornmeal with the seeds, a little at a time, in order to make the dough. Shape the dough into 2- to 3-inch-round pancakes. Fry them for about a minute on each side in vegetable oil until the cakes are brown on both sides.

Nasturtium Flower White Vinegar

Makes 8 ounces

This vinegar is a delicious marinade for meats, but it's just as tasty used as a dressing for salads.

- Nasturtium flowers, enough to loosely fill an 8-oz. glass jar
- 1 clove organic elephant garlic, thinly sliced, or 1 bunch garlic chives, chopped fine
- White balsamic vinegar, enough to fill an 8-oz. jar

Put the flowers and the garlic or chives into the glass jar and cover with balsamic vinegar. Let the jar sit for two weeks in a dark pantry before using as a marinade or dressing.

CHAPTER THIRTEEN

MAMA MIA
BEST-EVER MARINARA
SAUCE GARDEN

America's most popular backyard crop, tomatoes are the centerpiece of this cuisine garden. But, first, a little history of this versatile vegetable: Tomatoes were first cultivated, by the Incas, in the mountains of Peru and Chile. In the fifteenth century the Spanish exported the seeds to Europe, but it was another 300 years before tomatoes took center stage in Italian cuisine. Why? They had a bad rep. Experiments by European chefs determined that the leaves were poisonous, so at first tomatoes were persona non grata. Once people figured out that the delicious and robust round fruit was the edible part, the tomato's popularity took off.

New varieties made their way back to the Americas in the late 1700s and were quickly embraced by farmers. After large numbers of Italian immigrants arrived in the United States at the turn of the twentieth century, tomatoes entered America's culinary mainstream—all of which resulted in our love affair with Italian-style pasta sauce and pizza.

A tomato is ripe when it can easily be pulled from the vine. If it doesn't come off easily, it's not quite ready for eating. Tomatoes at the peak of their ripeness should be consumed immediately. And don't despair if a few get squishy and overripe—they're perfect for sauces and soups.

The great thing about growing your own tomatoes is that you can harvest them at the peak of their flavor, based on your own taste. I urge you to experiment with picking tomatoes at different stages of their growth (green tomatoes, for example, can be prepared in myriad delicious ways), but always remember—don't eat tomato leaves.

GROWING THE MARINARA SAUCE GARDEN

It's easy to grow great tomatoes and all the other ingredients you'll need to make the best marinara sauce you've ever tasted.

1. Plant a whole tomato bed at the same time, starting four weeks after the last spring frost. To save time and money, plant tomato and marigold seedlings right in the garden bed; as for the rest of the plants in this chapter, start them right in the bed from seed.

2. Cover the bed with a hoop house and keep the soil moist until the seeds germinate.

3. Once the seeds have germinated, remove the hoop house and install a trellis.

4. Mulch and water the bed as needed.

5. Harvest herbs and veggies in about 11 weeks.

What to Plant

In this garden, you will grow Tomatoes, Basil, Oregano, Chives, Scallions, and Marigolds.
Difficulty level Intermediate
Zones 4–10
Sunlight Full sun
Earliest planting date Four weeks after the last spring frost date

Garden Add-ons

Hoop House If you live in zones 4–8, protect your garden with a hoop house until average nighttime temperatures are in the 50s.
Trellis To learn how to build a simple trellis, see page 64.

PLANTS YOU NEED

Tomatoes
seedling
1 per 1 sq. ft.

Basil
seed or seedling
4 seeds or one
4–6-in. pot per
1 sq. ft.

Oregano
seed or seedling
1 pinch of seeds
or one 4–6-in.
pot per 4 sq. ft.

Chives
seed or seedling
16 seeds or one
4–6-in. pot per
1 sq. ft.

Scallions
seed
16 per 1 sq. ft.

Marigolds
seed or seedling
4 per 1 sq. ft.

CONTAINER & RAISED-BED GARDEN PLANS

WHAT YOU NEED

- Galvanized metal container or half wooded oak barrel, minimum 18 gal.
- Gravel or filler for proper drainage
- Organic potting soil
- One heirloom tomato plant, four marigold plants, four basil plants
- Compost, enough for a 1-in.-thick layer to cover the soil in the container

Container Garden

This is a fun container to grow on a patio or balcony, and it's perfect for beginners. You'll need a large container—at least 18 gallons. You can buy a galvanized metal container or a half oak barrel at your local garden center or building supplies store for between $20 and $40. For best results, plant your container garden with seedlings, not seeds.

HOW TO PREPARE THE CONTAINER

- Make at least 20 drainage holes in the bottom of the galvanized container using a large nail (¼ inch) and hammer.
- Fill the bottom with a 2-inch layer of ¾-inch gravel or a lighter substitute.
- Add organic potting soil, leaving 2 inches from the top of the container, and water thoroughly.

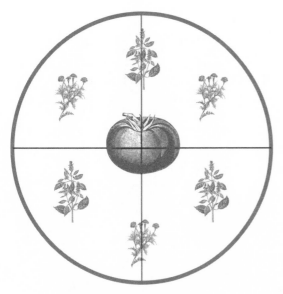

Even in small spaces like this container garden, it's important to include all of the designated plants, as each has an important role to play in companion planting. In many of my cuisine gardens, you can swap out favorites, but when it comes to tomatoes, nothing protects them better than basil and marigolds.

Container Garden Plan

PLANTING YOUR CONTAINER GARDEN

• Starting four weeks after the last spring frost, plant seedlings in the container according to the garden plan on the facing page. Water all seedlings in their containers before transplanting. Start by planting your tomato seedling in the center of the container, as deeply as you can, leaving at least 4 inches of the tomato seedling above the soil and pruning off any leaves that branch out below the soil.

• Plant the basil and marigolds in a ring around the tomato plant, making sure to space them evenly around the edge of the container.

• Water the soil thoroughly after planting, making sure that water drains out of the bottom of the container.

• Mulch the surface of the soil with an inch of compost.

• Install a tomato support and tie the tomato plants to it with string or jute (a strong natural fiber) as they grow.

HOW TO MAINTAIN YOUR CONTAINER GARDEN

• Containers dry out quickly and need to be watered almost daily.

• Once a week fertilize the soil with liquid fertilizer or compost tea.

• Add a thin layer of compost or worm castings (see pages 20–23) as mulch once a month.

Health Benefits Tomatoes are high in vitamin A and contain vitamin C, potassium, and calcium. Tomatoes are also rich in lycopene, a bright red pigment found in tomatoes and other red fruits that scientific studies say can aid in heart health and prevent prostate cancer. Canned, store-bought tomatoes are convenient, but they often contain a large amount of salt, sometimes 100 times the trace amounts found in fresh tomatoes. It really does pay to cook from scratch, using your own fresh, homegrown tomatoes.

Raised-Bed Garden Plans

The high-yielding, high-flavor marinara sauce garden is also a wonderful example of a permaculture environment, in which each of the plants, in addition to yielding foods that taste delicious together, helps the other plants thrive.

Whichever raised-bed plan you use, keep the tomatoes in the back so they can climb up the trellis. Plant the smaller herbs in front for best sun exposure.

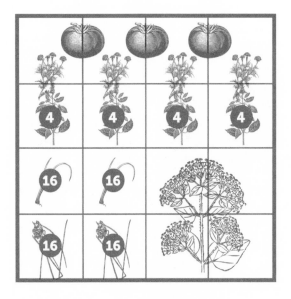

4 x 4 Plan

4 x 8 Plan

HEIRLOOM TOMATOES

Among the best heirlooms to grow, tomatoes come in a dazzling variety of shapes, colors, and sizes. I experiment with new heirloom varieties every year and replant the most successful ones. The varieties listed below are my favorites, based on flavor and abundance. Due to the shorter growing season in Boston, I have chosen smaller tomato varieties (seed to table in 70 days) that ripen sooner than some beefsteak varieties.

Start your own heirloom tomato seeds indoors, six to eight weeks before the average last frost date, and transplant them outside four weeks after the last frost.

Seed to table 70 days
Spacing for transplants 1 plant per square foot
Native to Central and South America

Patti's Picks

Royal Chico Tomato (*Lycopersicon lycopersicum*) A high-yield Roma type, this vigorous plant yields bright red, pear-shaped tomatoes that are perfect for making paste or canning. It is also resistant to disease, making it all the better for home gardens.

Cuor di Bue Tomato (*Solanum lycopersicum*) Considered an heirloom cultivar, this dark-pink to red, heart-shaped Italian variety can weigh up 12 ounces. The sweet-tasting fruit is great for sauce and tastes delicious right off the vine..

Marmande (*Solanum lycopersicum*) This slightly ribbed, pear-shaped heirloom yields a large beefsteak-type fruit, and like 'Royal Chico', it makes a great marinara sauce.

GROWING TOMATOES FROM SEEDS

Tomatoes are warm-weather crops; seedlings should be planted four weeks after the average last spring frost. Luckily, garden centers start stocking tomato seedlings when it's the right time to plant them outside. Start your own from seed indoors six to eight weeks before the average last frost date. This gives the seeds enough time to germinate and grow into plantable seedlings.

PLANTING TOMATO SEEDLINGS

Tomato seedlings that are over 4 inches tall should be planted deeply, leaving a minimum of 4 inches (of the plant) sticking out of the soil. All other vegetable plants should be planted no deeper than the soil line in the container from which you are transplanting the seedlings, keeping the stem and plant above the soil line. Tomato plants are the exception to this rule. Roots will grow from the stem of the plant, so planting a tomato plant nice and deep will help it grow a larger root ball that can access more water for juicier tomatoes and make the plant sturdier.

1. In the center of 1 square foot of soil, dig a hole deep enough so that nearly the entire main stem of the tomato seedling is under the soil line, with only the top of the plant above the soil.

2. Clip off all leaves and smaller side branches that will fall below the soil line and put the plant in the hole.

3. Fill the hole with soil, and water thoroughly until at least the top 6 inches of soil are saturated with water.

GETTING BIGGER PLANTS INTO THE GROUND

As an alternative to the traditional hole method described above, you can use a system called *trenching* to get plants that are more than 10 inches high into the ground. The trenching method has two advantages: You don't need to dig a deep hole, and the entire length of the plant's root system grows in the upper, nutrient-rich layer of soil. In the spring, the shallow layers of the soil warm quickly, promoting the plant's growth.

1. Dig a 5-inch-deep horizontal trench—as long as the plant's roots and stem— diagonally across 1 square foot in the garden.

2. Remove all the leaves from the plant except the top cluster.

3. Lay the tomato plant on its side in the trench.

4. Cover the root ball and the bare stem with soil up to the top cluster of leaves.

5. When you have filled in the trench, the part of the plant above ground will be lying on the soil, but don't worry, it will grow upward in about a week.

6. Water the newly planted seedling thoroughly until the top 6 inches of soil are saturated with water.

7. The tip of the plant will gradually point up and grow.

8. Support the plant with a tomato cage (you can purchase these simple supports for as little as $13 at your local garden store).

PRUNING TOMATOES

Pruning is necessary to maximize the production of more fruit, but you need to prune judiciously. Prune tomato plants throughout the growing season to help ward off pests and diseases. Pruning also improves airflow around your the plants, keeping them dry. Begin pruning tomato plants once the first set of flowers blossom. Prune all branches below the lowest set of flowers, and make sure your plants are properly attached to a trellis or tomato support. As your plants grow, pinch off all the suckers (stems that grow in the V space between the main stem and the branches of the plants). However, if tomatoes are exposed to too much sunlight, as they are ripening, sunscald on the fruit can occur. The best way to avoid sunscald is to not over-prune the plants—the fruit needs to be shaded by some branches and leaves.

PESTS & DISEASES

Tomatoes can develop brown spots—called *blossom end rot*—when watering is uneven and inconsistent. Fruit with blossom end rot is no longer viable and should be taken off the vine and discarded. (See Chapter Two for more information about preventing diseases, deterring pests, and treating infected tomato plants.)

HARVESTING TOMATOES

Your tomatoes will start off green and eventually begin to change color as they ripen. A ripe tomato that's ready to eat will be soft to the touch, but not squishy, and there should be little to no green left on the skin. Using pruning shears, cut the ripe tomato at the stem. Harvest only as many tomatoes as you plan to eat at your next meal. If you have a lot of ripe tomatoes—more than you can consume (good job, by the way)—pick and share them with others, or use them for their seeds, which you can save for next year. You can also preserve tomatoes that you're not using or giving away by canning them or making them into sauce.

SAVING TOMATO SEEDS

This saving method can be used for any vegetable seed that has a fleshy or gel coating around the seed. Save seeds from the tastiest varieties of tomatoes that have yielded the most prolific harvest. These seeds, when properly stored, can be kept for at least five to seven years. (Older seeds will have low germination rates but may produce some tomato plants.)

1. Select a few healthy, ripe tomatoes that taste great. If you have multiple plants of the same type, pick fruit from each of them.

2. Using tape and a marker, label each container with the variety of seed you are saving.

3. Squeeze seeds from the tomatoes into the plastic containers, filling each container no more than half full.

4. Place containers with seeds and juice out of the sun, in a cool place such as a shed or garage. Your containers will emit odors and attract fruit flies. That is good.

5. Check the containers daily, but don't stir the contents. Within five days a white film (fungus) will have grown on the surface of the liquid.

6. Skim off the white fungus with a spoon. Rinse the seeds in the containers with cool water until the water runs clear, using a small metal strainer. Be careful not to lose any seeds.

7. Drain the remaining clear water, and lay out the seeds on a paper plate or paper towel, arranging them in a layer one-seed thick.

8. Allow the seeds to dry, out of the sun, in a shed or garage.

9. Once the seeds are dry, store them in sandwich bags or envelopes labeled with the variety and date.

HEIRLOOM HERBS

You can start these herbs from seed or with seedlings. They not only go well with tomatoes in an endless number of recipes, but also grow well together in the garden. Few pests or diseases affect these culinary herbs. As a matter of fact, aromatic herbs are used as companion plants to other vegetables, such as eggplants and sweet peppers, and are used in many organic insecticidal sprays to deter garden pests.

BASIL

The perfect companion to your tomatoes, basil is used as a flavorful additive in many cuisines, especially in Italian dishes. Most folks would agree that Italian food just wouldn't be the same without basil. During the Middle Ages, basil was used for its various medicinal properties—to cure headaches, eye diseases, and stomachache.

Seed to table 75–80 days
Spacing for seeds 4 per square foot
Spacing for transplants One 4- to 6-inch pot per square foot
Native to Southeast Asian, India

Patti's Picks

Genovese Basil (*Ocimum basilicum* 'Genovese Gigante') A cultivar of sweet basil, Genovese basil is one of the most popular culinary herbs, particularly for its use in pesto and garlic-flavored dishes.

Fine Verde Basil (*Ocimum basilicum* 'Piccolo') The very small leaves on this compact plant make it a great herb to grow in small spaces and containers. Its spicy flavor and sweet aroma make a distinct contribution to Italian cuisine.

Lemon Basil (*Ocimum basilicum* var. *citriodorum*) This small-leaved plant is not as bold-looking as Genovese or large-leaf basil, but its aroma and taste are outstanding. Used in pesto half and half with Genovese basil, it provides a delicious kick of lemon every few bites or so. This fragrant basil is also great in tea and potpourris.
Height 12–18 inches

For more information on growing basil see page 146.

OREGANO

This perennial culinary herb is a member of the mint family. Although it has similar growth habits, oregano tastes completely different from mint and is not used in the same way in the kitchen. Oregano has an earthy flavor and helps tame the fruitiness of tomatoes in marinara sauce. Use it fresh or dried to season soups and sauces.

Seed to table 56–70 days
Spacing for seeds 1 pinch of seeds per 4 square feet
Spacing for transplants One 4- to 6-inch pot per 4 square feet
Native to Mediterranean

Patti's Picks

Oregano (*Origanum vulgare*) Oregano is a staple of Italian-American cuisine. Its popularity in the United States dates back to World War II, when American soldiers, who had grown fond of the "pizza herb," brought it back home with them from Italy. Oregano can also be used medicinally, particularly for stomach ailments—and it's high in antioxidants.

CHIVES

Chives are a perennial plant and part of the onion family—in fact, they are the smallest of the edible onion species, but because they pack in a lot of flavor, they are used as a seasoning. Chives also have insect-repelling properties, which make them welcome additions to the garden.

Seed to table 77–80 days
Spacing for seeds 16 per square foot
Spacing for transplants One 4- to 6-inch pot per square foot
Native to Europe and Asia

Patti's Pick

Garlic Chives (*Allium tuberosum*) This cold-hardy variety of the onion family has a strong garlic flavor. The flowers are scented and taste like garlic too.

Common Chives (*Allium schoenoprasum*)   These fast-growing chives are cold-hardy and have a sweet, subtle onion flavor. They are easy to grow and can be harvested year-round indoors if you grow them in a container.

HARVESTING HERBS

• Harvest herbs regularly by cutting off the tops of the plants. This will keep herbs growing and prevent them from flowering too early. Herbs taste best before they start flowering.

• Use fresh herbs throughout the growing season or preserve them by drying or freezing them.

• In the fall, once your herbs start dying and average nighttime temperatures are in the 50s, remove the herbs from the garden or cover them with a hoop house to extend your culinary herb harvest into early winter.

• See page 73 for more information on growing, harvesting, and preserving culinary herbs, as well as saving herb seeds.

HEIRLOOM SCALLIONS

Growing true onions takes a long time—sometimes more than 100 days—before the bulb is ready to harvest, and onions can take up lots of garden space if you want a plentiful harvest. But you can still grow onions in small spaces from seed and eat them when they are green. These immature onions are commonly called scallions. Sow onion seeds in the garden about ¼ inch deep and keep the soil moist until they germinate, then allow the soil to dry between waterings.

Seed to table 45 days
Spacing for seeds 16 per square foot
Native to Asia

Patti's Pick

Tropeana Lunga Onion (*Allium cepa* var. *cepa*)   This red onion variety is popular with Mediterranean chefs and can be picked and used like a scallion by trimming the top or by harvesting when the bulb is the size of a nickel. It should be consumed quickly since the sweet bulbs do not keep particularly well. It's widely grown throughout the Mediterranean.

HARVESTING SCALLIONS

Start harvesting scallions when the onions are still green by cutting off the tops and leaving at least 2 inches of the spear sticking out of the soil. When they are the size of a pencil, pull the entire scallion out of the soil, roots and all. Wash off any soil under cool water and cut off the roots before eating the scallion. At this stage, these green onions taste sweet and crunchy when eaten raw.

PESTS & DISEASES

Root rot is one of the diseases to look out for when growing onions. It can come about if onions get too much water after they've germinated. To prevent this, make sure to let the soil dry out between waterings. Pests, such as aphids, can strike, but scallions are a quick-growing crop, and if you harvest regularly this shouldn't be a problem.

SAVING SEEDS

In order to save seeds you will need to let some of your onions continue to grow, flower, and set (go to) seed, which means that you can't eat all that you grow. If black seeds fall easily from the flower, then the seeds are ready to be harvested. Store the seeds in a cool, dark place in a glass jar until early spring. I recommend saving seeds from anything you grow, whether it's edible or not, and using them in your garden the next year. You'll have more than you can use, so share the seeds with friends and neighbors.

MARIGOLDS

Companion planting marigolds in a raised bed adds color to your garden and helps keep garden pests away—the natural way. Marigolds have a natural repellant in their roots that deter microscopic pests that can feed on the roots of vegetable plants, such as your tomatoes (killing the harvest). Marigolds can grow to be quite large; I like to plant small dwarf varieties that won't take over my garden. Marigolds are easy-to-grow annuals. If you steadily pinch off old flowers throughout the growing season and discard them, they'll keep blooming until the first hard frost, when they'll start to die off. Replant in the spring from seed and regularly remove any yellow or brown leaves and stems to prevent disease.

SAVING SEEDS

In order to save marigold seeds, stop pruning spent flower buds from the plant and allow them to set seed. Pick off spent blossoms, once they have set seed, and separate the seeds from the dried flower petals. Store the seeds in a glass jar in a cool dark place. Don't forget to label the jar with they type of seed it contains and also put the date on the jar.

Seed to table 60 days
Spacing for seeds 4 per square foot
Spacing for transplants 4 per square foot
Native to The Americas

Patti's Pick

Petite Mixed French Marigold (*Tagetes patula*) Boasting a colorful mix of orange, yellow, red, and variegated flowers, this compact dwarf marigold adds visual delight to your garden.

RECIPES FOR AN HEIRLOOM TOMATO GARDEN

Now it's time for you to step out of the garden and into the kitchen. Get your aprons on! Here are a few of my favorite, easy recipes that use ingredients from this versatile garden. Be sure to try the recipe for the marinara sauce—it really is the "best ever." *Buon appetito!*

Mama Mia Best-Ever Marinara Sauce

Makes about 10 cups of sauce

The secret to this recipe is the freshness of the ingredients, especially lots of Royal Chico paste tomatoes and a whole bulb of garlic!

10	lbs. ripe tomatoes, such as Royal Chico paste tomatoes
¼	cup extra-virgin olive oil, or more, depending on taste
3	cups finely chopped onions and onion tops
1	whole bulb garlic, finely chopped
4	tbsp. sugar, or to taste
1	cup minced fresh oregano
2	cups minced fresh basil
	Salt and pepper, to taste

Roughly chop the tomatoes and run them through a food mill (run the pulp and skins multiple times through the mill until all the juice is squeezed out). Heat 2 tablespoons of the olive oil in a large saucepan and sauté the onions over medium heat for 3 minutes, then add the garlic and cook over moderate heat, until soft and golden brown. Add the tomato pulp and juices and bring the mixture to a boil. Add the remainder of the olive oil, or more, according to your taste, then add the sugar and oregano. Lower the heat to medium and simmer, uncovered, for 30 minutes, stirring occasionally. Lower the heat, stir, and allow the sauce to thicken for 15 more minutes. You may need to cook the sauce a little longer, depending on how thick you like it (the sauce should reduce to about one half to one quarter the amount of liquid you started with). Mix in the basil last, a couple minutes before serving. Add salt and pepper, to taste.

Heirloom Tomato Salad

Serves four to six

Nothing says "summer" better than this fresh salad!

4–6	medium ripe heirloom tomatoes
20	leaves of basil
2	tbsp. extra-virgin olive oil
2	tbsp. balsamic vinegar
	Salt and pepper, to taste

Cut the tomatoes into bite-size pieces and place them in a large bowl. Tear the basil leaves and add them to the bowl. Drizzle olive oil and vinegar over the mixture. Add salt and pepper. Mix thoroughly and serve.

Green Tomato Soup

Serves four to six

This summery soup is delicious served either hot or cold.

2	tbsp. extra-virgin olive oil
1	bay leaf
1	cup thinly sliced scallions
½	cup minced garlic chives
2	lbs. green (unripe) tomatoes, chopped
1	cup low-sodium chicken or vegetable broth
2	cups water
	Salt and pepper, to taste

Heat the olive oil in a large, heavy saucepan over medium heat until hot. Add the bay leaf; then, stirring occasionally, add and sauté scallions and garlic chives until the scallions are tender and lightly browned, about 5 minutes. Add tomatoes and sauté for one minute; then add broth and water, and simmer, partially covered, until the tomatoes are tender, about 15 to 20 minutes. Season with salt and pepper.

Bruschetta with Tomatoes, Basil, & Chives

Makes 24–30 small slices. Serves six to ten as an appetizer
or three or four for lunch.

I use plum tomatoes for bruschetta because there are fewer seeds
and less juice.

There's nothing like a savory mix of tomatoes, basil, garlic, and
chives on thin slices of gently oiled, toasted bread.

1½–2	lbs. Royal Chico tomatoes
2	cloves garlic, minced
2	tbsp. plus ¼ cup extra-virgin olive oil
1	tsp. white balsamic vinegar
1	cup chopped basil leaves
1	tbsp. finely chopped garlic chives
	Salt and pepper, to taste
1	loaf Italian wheat bread

Preheat your oven to 450° F. Make sure the top rack is in place. Bring
a large saucepan of water to a boil. Remove the pan from the heat
and gently submerge all the tomatoes in the hot water for 1 minute.
Drain the tomatoes and remove the skins under cold running water.
Cut the tomatoes into quarters and remove all seeds and juice. Chop
the tomatoes finely. In a large bowl, combine the tomatoes, garlic, 2
tablespoons of the olive oil, and the vinegar. Add the chopped basil
and garlic chives. Add salt and pepper. Slice the bread on a diagonal
into ½-inch-thick slices. With a pastry brush, coat one side of each
slice with olive oil. Place the bread slices on a cooking tray, olive oil
side down, then place the tray on the top rack of the oven for 5 or 6
minutes until the bread begins to turn golden brown. Place the bread
slices on a serving platter, olive oil side up. Spoon some tomato topping on each slice of bread and serve immediately before the bread
gets soggy.

Sun-Dried Tomatoes

Makes about 1 pint

For this recipe, you'll need an electric food dehydrator. These machines are great for drying vegetables and fruit, and well worth the price of about $100. Sun-dried tomatoes are a convenient staple to have on hand. A little bit goes a long way to add an intense burst of tomato-y flavor to a variety of recipes. Sun-dried tomatoes are easy to make and store, and they taste so much better than store-bought versions.

6   lbs. Roma or plum tomatoes

    Salt

½   cup chopped garlic chives

    Olive oil, enough to fill half of a pint-size jar

Slice the tomatoes in half, lengthwise, and scoop out just the seeds with a spoon. Make another slit lengthwise on the skin side of each tomato slice. Sprinkle lightly with salt and place the tomato halves on dehydrator trays skin side down. The drying process can take 8 hours or more. Check the tomatoes periodically and remove any that are dry. The tomatoes are done when they are still flexible and not crunchy. Once you've finished drying all your tomatoes, put them in a large bowl and mix in the garlic chives. Fill a pint-size jar halfway with olive oil. Add as much of the tomato and garlic chives mixture as you can to the jar of olive oil. You can store the mixture in your refrigerator for up to three months. You can also vacuum-seal and store the dried tomatoes in the freezer for six to nine months.

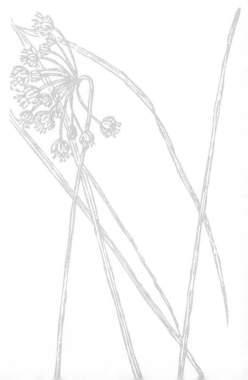

Genovese & Lemon Basil Pesto

Makes 4 cups

Most recipes for pesto call for salt, but I don't add any to this lemony variation on the traditional pesto. The salt in the Parmesan cheese is enough for me. It's remarkably easy to omit the salt in this and so many other recipes. I urge you to cut back on salt, at least in your own cooking. You won't miss it. Toss this delicious pesto with your favorite pasta or a combination of veggies, or spread it lightly over grilled fish or chicken breasts.

4	cloves organic garlic
¼	cup pine nuts or walnuts
1	cup fresh Genovese basil leaves
1	cup fresh lemon basil leaves
1½	cups extra-virgin olive oil
1	cup grated Parmesan cheese (Parmigiano-Reggiano is especially good)
1	tsp. fresh lemon juice or 1 tsp. lemon zest (optional)
	Ground pepper

Place the garlic and pine nuts or walnuts into a food processor. (Garlic freaks like me can add as much garlic as they want—this recipe is a tamer version of what I make for my family.) Add the Genovese and lemon basil leaves and start drizzling some of the olive oil into the processor and press the pulse setting. With the machine still running, add the cheese and lemon juice or zest, if you're using it, and gradually drizzle in the last of the oil, until the mixture reaches the consistency you like. Add pepper to taste and sprinkle on a little extra grated cheese, if you like.

Spicy Bloody Mary

Makes 2 drinks

You can store this delicious beverage in the refrigerator for up to a week if you don't drink it right away. Leave out the vodka and you have a deliciously refreshing summer drink. You can add any garnish you like, whether it's a lemon wedge, a stalk of fresh celery, or a crunchy pickled green bean from one of your raised beds.

- 1   medium-large tomato, chopped

     Juice of 1 lemon

- 2   cups ice-cold water

- 4   oz. vodka

     Sea salt

     Ground pepper

- 1   pinch dried oregano or 1 tsp. freshly chopped basil

     Tabasco sauce

- 1   lemon, cut into wedges

Blend the tomatoes and the juice of one lemon in a food mill, juicer, or blender. Empty the contents into a bowl. Add ice water and mix. Add vodka and seasoning to taste. Serve over ice with a lemon wedge.

CHAPTER FOURTEEN

LATIN-CARIBBEAN SOFRITO GARDEN

I've written this final chapter as a spicy valentine to Puerto Rico, where my family comes from, and as an invitation to try some of the wonderful, tropical tastes I grew up with and enjoyed at my mother's table. Native foods of South America and the Caribbean Islands, from bananas and coconuts to seafood, dominate Latin-Caribbean cooking, which has also been influenced by the cuisines of Africa, Spain, India, and Asia. But most of all, Latin-Caribbean cuisine, including Puerto Rico's, tastes best when it is made from scratch with fresh ingredients from the garden.

Living in New England, I can't grow passion fruit or coconuts or sugarcane. I can, however, grow onions, peppers, and cilantro, the main ingredients in *sofrito*—a marinade that is beloved in Latin-Caribbean cooking and used for seasoning fish, beef, pork, poultry, and even rice. Every Christmas my family and many other Latin-Caribbean families feast on *pernil* (roasted pork), which is marinated with sofrito. Luckily, the ingredients for this traditional marinade can be grown just about everywhere.

A multitude of side dishes can be served along with the pernil, but my favorite is one of the simplest—rice and beans—also called *arroz con gandules*. This delicious side dish is essential to my family's Christmas holiday table. (My mom's recipe is on page 241). *Gandules* are grown on a tree in the tropics, so I can't grow them in New England, let alone in a raised bed, but I can grow red kidney beans instead. So after some experimenting, I've put together a Latin-Caribbean culinary bed that includes these essential ingredients and more. For those of you who want to spice it up a bit in the kitchen, the garden plans in this chapter will deliver plenty of fireworks, not to mention memorable flavors, and dishes that will, hopefully, become traditional for your celebrations as well. *Buen provecho!*

GROWING THE LATIN-CARIBBEAN GARDEN

I've tested the veggies and herbs recommended for the sofrito garden, and they grow well in raised beds. They also have shorter growing seasons than other varieties that are used to make sofrito. But there are lots of other things you can make with the vegetables in this bed, and I'll show you how. You've learned a lot about growing some of these veggies in previous chapters, so some of this will be old hat for you by now.

Harvest times start at 50 days for hot peppers and at 60 or 70 days for the other veggies in this garden.

What to Plant

In this garden, you will grow Beans, Tomatoes, Bell peppers, Hot peppers, Bunching onions (scallions), Marigolds, and Cilantro.
Difficulty level Intermediate
Zones All
Sunlight Full sun
Earliest planting date from seed (*for beans, bunching onions, cilantro, and marigolds*) Four weeks before the average last (spring) frost date.
Earliest planting date from transplants (*for tomatoes and peppers*) Two weeks after the average last (spring) frost date.

Garden Add-ons

Hoop House If you live in zone 7 or colder, protect your garden with a hoop house until average nighttime temperatures are in the 50s.
Trellis To learn how to build a garden trellis, see page 64.

PLANTS YOU NEED

Beans
seed
5 per 1 sq. ft.

Tomatoes
seedling
1 per 1 sq. ft.

Bell Pepper
seedling
1 per 2 sq. ft.

Hot Pepper
seedling
1 per 2 sq. ft.

Marigolds
seed or seedling
4 per 1 sq. ft.

Cilantro
seed or seedling
9 seeds or one
4–6-in. pot per
1 sq. ft.

Bunching Onions
seed
16 per 1 sq. ft.

WHAT YOU NEED

- A large container, at least 24 in. in diameter, with drainage holes. A galvanized metal container or half oak barrel works really well, but almost any material will do—clay, plastic, or metallic pots; barrels; planter boxes, etc.
- Planter insert or other filler, like gravel
- Enough organic potting soil to fill the container
- Plants
- A plant support, such as a trellis
- Enough compost to mulch a 1-in. layer on top of the soil

CONTAINER & RAISED-BED GARDEN PLANS

Latin-Caribbean Sofrito Container Garden

The veggies in this garden do well in containers, whether you use a planter box, a wood barrel, or clay, plastic, or metallic pots. Use a nail to hammer between 10 and 20 drainage holes in the bottom of the container—enough for good drainage, but not so many that the integrity of the bottom is damaged. A planter can be large and heavy to move, so be sure to place it where you want it to be before filling it up. It's best to use a filler that's lightweight and airy in the bottom of your container. For good drainage, try using a product called Better Than Rocks or other types of fibrous container filler. Lightweight fillers like these will help you save money on potting soil, too. Simply layer the filler in the bottom of your container and place a cloth (such as landscape fabric or weed barrier cloth) over the filler to keep soil from trickling down into the gaps. I also like to use planter inserts from Ups-A-Daisy (www.ups-a-daisy.com) because they can fit into many different kinds of containers and also eliminate the need for filler materials.

PLANTING THE CONTAINER GARDEN

1. Place the container where you want it to be for the growing season.

2. Fill the bottom of the container with at least 2 inches of gravel or other filler.

3. Fill the container with organic potting soil, leaving at least 2 inches from the lip of the container.

4. Water the soil thoroughly before planting.

5. Start by planting in the middle of the container, according to the diagram shown at left, then spread out from there.

Container Plan

6. Water the soil again and add a 1-inch-thick layer of compost as mulch on top of the soil around the plants.

7. Water one more time, and set up drip irrigation if you're using it. (See pages 16–18 for information about drip irrigation.)

8. Install a plant support (such as a trellis) for the tomato plant.

9. Water the container regularly as needed. Containers dry out quickly, so water daily, if necessary.

Raised-Bed Garden Plans

As always when planting to one of my raised-bed garden plans, feel free to substitute family favorites for some of the vegetables in my plan. There are multiple squares for each plant, so try experimenting with a few varieties of each to find out which ones taste best to you and which grow best in your garden.

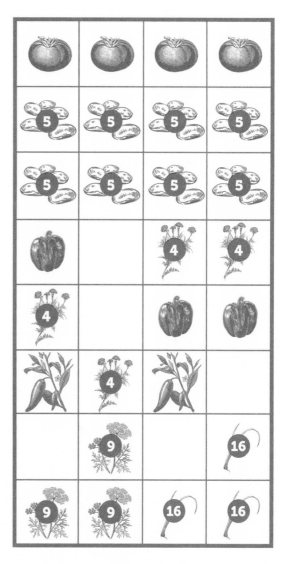

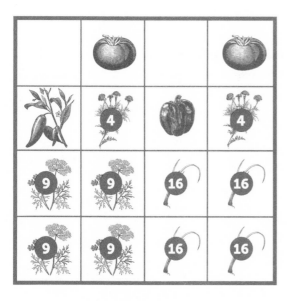

4 x 4 Plan

4 x 8 Plan

BEANS

Beans are incredibly easy to grow, they can be eaten many different ways, and they're healthy for you. Immature bean pods can be harvested and eaten raw or cooked like string beans. You can also allow the pod to grow until the bean on the inside is mature and ready for shelling. In Latin-Caribbean cuisine, the beans are dried and stored and used in rice dishes, bean salads, and as a side dish to be served over rice. For many vegetarians, beans are a satisfying meat substitute because they're high in protein. In addition, the fiber in beans is great for digestion, helps prevent heart disease, and lowers cholesterol.

Bean plants are either bush varieties or vining varieties. Bean seeds are simply the dried version of the edible bean. Plant beans from seed, 1 inch deep, two weeks after the last frost. If you're growing a vining variety, use a trellis or a beanpole to support it; install it when you sow your bean seeds. Keep the soil moist once you've planted your seeds. If outdoor conditions are right, your beans will sprout in a few days. As they grow, make sure to train the vines to climb on the beanpole. Anywhere you see a flower there's potential for a bean pod to form.

Seed to table 70–100 days
Spacing for seeds 5 per square foot
Native to the Americas

Patti's Pick

Red Kidney Bean (Phaseolus vulgaris) This kidney-shaped bean is sometimes referred to as a red bean or chili bean. It makes a delicious, classic Caribbean side dish served with rice or mixed with rice in a salad.
Height up to 12 feet (vines)

PESTS & DISEASES

Prevent pests and diseases by removing any yellow or brown leaves and discarding them. When you're watering, make sure to water the soil, not the leaves of the plant.

HARVESTING & SAVING BEANS

Once the bean pods begin drying out in late summer, stop watering the soil around the plants. When most of the pods are a tan color, pick off all the pods and pull out the plants. Separate the beans from the pods and allow them to dry in a cool, dark place. Once the beans are dry, store them in a glass jar until you want to use them. Before using the beans, soak them in cool water for at least 5 hours and boil them for 10 minutes. NOTE: Red kidney beans should not be eaten raw because they contain the toxin *phytohaemagglutinin,* which can make you sick.

TOMATOES

Native to South America, tomatoes were spread throughout the Americas and the Caribbean and eaten for centuries before Europeans landed in the Caribbean. Before that time, tomatoes were eaten like a fruit. When Africans arrived in the area, they brought a stewing culture with them, and tomatoes were used to round out the flavor in sauces.

Start your own heirloom tomato seeds indoors, beginning six to eight weeks before the last frost, and transplant outside four weeks after the last frost.

Seed to table 70–85 days
Spacing for transplants 1 plant per square foot
Native to Central and South America

GROWING TOMATOES FROM SEEDS

If you want a challenge, you can start your own plants from seed indoors, six to eight weeks before the average last frost date. This gives the seeds enough time to germinate and grow into plantable seedlings that are at least 4 inches tall.

PLANTING TOMATO SEEDLINGS

Tomatoes like it warm, so seedlings should be planted four weeks after the average last spring frost. Once the climate conditions are right for tomatoes to grow, you'll find them at your local garden center. If you order seedlings online, they will be delivered to you at the appropriate growing time for your area.

Tomato seedlings that are more than 4 inches tall should be planted deeply, leaving a minimum of 4 inches of the plant sticking out of the soil. Roots will grow from the stem of a tomato plant, so planting it nice and deep will help it grow a larger root ball that can access more water for juicier tomatoes and a sturdier plant.

1. In the center of 1 square foot of soil, dig a hole deep enough so that nearly the entire main stem of the tomato seedling is under the soil line, with only the top 4 inches of the plant above the soil.

2. Clip off all leaves and smaller side branches that will fall below the soil line, and put the plant in the hole.

3. Fill the hole with soil, and water thoroughly until at least the top 6 inches of soil are saturated with water.

Patti's Pick

Santa Cruz Cada Tomato (*Lycopersicon esculentum*) This variety yields a midsize red tomato with few seeds and solid, sweet flesh. It is highly versatile—perfect for marinades, pastes, sauces, and canning as well as salads, or eaten right off the plant.
Height 6-10 feet

PRUNING TOMATOES

Pruning is necessary to maximize the production of more fruit, but you need to prune judiciously. Prune tomato plants throughout the growing season to help ward off pests and diseases. Pruning also improves airflow around the plants, keeping them dry. Begin pruning tomato plants once the first set of flowers blossom. Prune all branches below the lowest set of flowers, and make sure your plants are properly attached to a trellis or tomato support. As your plants grow, pinch off all the suckers (stems that grow in the V space between the main stem and the branches of the plants).

If tomatoes are exposed to too much sunlight as they are ripening, the fruit can experience sunscald. The best way to avoid this is not to over-prune the plants—the fruit needs to be shaded by some branches and leaves.

PESTS & DISEASES

Tomatoes can develop brown spots—called *blossom end rot*—when watering is uneven and inconsistent. Fruit with blossom end rot is no longer viable and should be taken off the vine and discarded. Refer to Chapter Two for more information on preventing diseases and deterring pests as well as treating infected tomato plants.

HARVESTING TOMATOES

Your tomatoes will start off green and eventually begin changing color until they are red. This means they are ripe and ready to be eaten. A ripe tomato will be soft to the touch, but not squishy, and should have little to no green left. Using pruning shears, cut the ripe tomato at the stem. Harvest the number of tomatoes you plan to use for your next meal. If you have a lot of ripe tomatoes, more than you can use, pick them and share them with others. Alternatively, you can save the seeds from the fruit for planting next year or preserve and can the tomatoes for use throughout the year.

SAVING TOMATO SEEDS

See page 214 for information about saving tomato seeds.

PEPPERS

Peppers are a key ingredient in Latin-Caribbean cuisine because they add depth of flavor to just about everything. Growing peppers is easy and very similar to growing eggplants. If you live in a warm climate, you can start pepper seeds right in your garden bed because there's no danger of frost and the conditions are perfect for the seeds to germinate in the soil. Just keep them moist until they sprout—in about 10 to 20 days. If you live in a cool climate, you'll need to start seeds indoors six to eight weeks before the average last spring frost date. You can also buy organic seedlings online or at your local garden center.

Seed to table 60–95 days
Spacing for transplants 1 plant per 2 square feet
Native to South America

PLANTING PEPPERS

1. Make sure your seedling is well watered before planting.

2. Dig a hole in the center of the planting square.

3. Remove the plant from the container and place the plant in the hole no deeper than it was grown in the container.

4. Fill the hole with soil, water, and mulch. Then water the soil again.

5. Add a plant support (6-foot wire cages work well).

6. Water frequently for the first four to six weeks while the plant establishes itself. Then allow the soil to dry out between waterings.

Patti's Pick

California Wonder Green Pepper (*Capsicum annuum*) This is one of the most delicious and versatile homegrown green peppers. It tastes great when eaten fresh in salads or in my sofrito recipe (see page 239).
Height 3 to 4 feet tall and 2 feet wide

PESTS & DISEASES

Companion planting this garden with marigolds and cilantro (see pages 236–237) will be one of your best defenses against pests and diseases. Make sure that you water properly, being careful not to water the leaves of the plant, and don't allow leaves to collect around the bottom of the plant. The best thing to do if you notice a problem is to remove the affected plant before it infects the whole garden.

HARVESTING PEPPERS

Peppers can be harvested whenever you need them. Varieties that change color as they mature—for example, to red, orange, or yellow—will be ready to be picked once they turn that color. Peppers are still delicious even when they're green. Just clip off the pepper at the stem, eat it raw, or use it in myriad cooked preparations.

SAVING PEPPER SEEDS

Saving pepper seeds is easy. Whenever you eat a pepper, put the seeds on a paper plate and let them dry in a cool dark place. Once they are dry, store them in a glass jar and use them to start your pepper plants indoors in the winter. Also, you can share the seeds with others!

HOT PEPPERS

Hot peppers can be grown with lots of success and with little care, although they do best in warm climates, where the heat helps make them really hot. I've had good luck growing different kinds of hot peppers in the Northeast, too. No matter where you grow them, these little powerhouses provide plenty of vitamins your body needs, including vitamins A, C, K, B6, and folates, as well as vitamin C. Hot peppers also help lower blood pressure.

Seed to table 50 days (with a transplant)
Spacing for transplants 1 per 2 square feet
Native to Central and South America

Patti's Pick

Habanero (*Capiscum chinense*) The traditional hot pepper of the Caribbean islands and Latin America, habanero (also known as Scotch bonnet) can vary in color from green to yellow to pink, and though they are relatively small—at 1–2½ inches in length and 1–2 inches in diameter—these peppers really pack a punch. They may not be the hottest pepper known to man; still, they're about all I can take! The Scoville scale, a heat index that measures the spicy heat of a chili pepper, based on the amount of capsaicin it contains, ranges from 0 (no "significant" heat; examples are bell peppers and *aji dulce* peppers) to 1,500,000—2,000,000 (a category that includes the legendary ghost pepper). The orange habanero pepper's heat rating of 150,000 to 325,000 puts it in the top 10 on the Scoville scale. Use these peppers to taste in your cooking, and you'll discover an exciting, new dimension of spiciness and heat.

Height 3–4 feet

HARVESTING HOT PEPPERS

Use gloves when harvesting habaneros or any hot pepper, because they can really sting and burn if you rub your eyes with your hands. Not fun. Hot peppers can be harvested green, but their heat intensity increases as they ripen and turn bright orange. Some varieties turn red, yellow, and even white at the height of ripeness.

HOW HOT IS HOT?

Hot peppers (chili peppers) are measured on the Scoville unit scale, named after Wilbur L. Scoville, a chemist who devised the scale to measure the heat factor—the amount of capsaicin—in hot peppers. Orange habanero peppers are rated 150,000–325,000 Scoville units. The hottest pepper is the Trinidad Moruga scorpion, which is rated at 900,000–1,463,700 Scoville heat units. (For more on peppers and their hotness, see **ushotstuff.com**.)

BUNCHING ONIONS/SCALLIONS

Bunching onions (*Allium fistulosum*), also called scallions, are mild and can be used fresh, like any other green onion. (Scallions are simply onions that are harvested before they've grown a bulb.) Bunching onions are easy to grow and adapt well to many different climates.

Seed to table Scalllions: 60 days; green onions: 120 days.
Spacing for seeds 16 per square foot
Native to Asia

Patti's Pick

White Sweet Spanish Valencia Bunching Onions (*Allium fistulosum*). This quick-growing, sweet, and flavorful variety does not form a bulb and is harvested and eaten green. Start these bunching onions from seed outside, right in the garden, as early in the season as possible. They're cold-hardy but can take up to 21 days to germinate, so if you're planting bunching onions outside in a raised bed, a hoop house is a good option. Keep the soil moist until the seeds germinate (in 7–10 days), then water as needed.

Height 12–18 inches

HARVESTING BUNCHING ONIONS

To harvest bunching onions, just clip off the bright green tops when they reach a height of 8–10 inches. Keep the onions growing into late summer or early fall and then harvest the entire onion root.

COMPANION PLANTS/ MARIGOLDS & CILANTRO

Companion plants play a protective role in the garden, helping vegetable plants stay healthy through a good harvest. In the Latin-Caribbean garden, marigolds and cilantro are the companion plants. Wherever nightshade plants such as tomatoes, eggplants, and peppers are grown, it's always a great idea to plant marigolds and culinary herbs alongside them to ward off harmful garden insects. I companion-plant dwarf marigolds to help control insects, such as aphids and tomato hornworms, and to kill harmful nematodes that live in the soil.

As with most if not all types of plants, marigolds come in different colors and sizes. My favorites are the dwarf varieties because they stay small. These mini marigolds are easy to start from seed indoors, but I love starting them outside in early spring, right in the bed, before I plant any edibles. I cover the bed with a hoop house and in a few days the seeds germinate.

Marigolds are readily available at garden centers in lots of solid colors and as multicolored flowers in varying shades of red, orange, and yellow. For every tomato, pepper, or eggplant in the bed, I plant at least three marigolds.

Marigolds can be very large, so I don't recommend planting anything other than the dwarf variety. Throughout the growing season pinch off spent blossoms from the plant to promote more blooms. You can prevent diseases by regularly removing any yellow or brown leaves and stems. Marigolds are annuals, so once it gets cold the plants will die off and you'll need to plant them again the next year.

As a culinary herb and companion plant, cilantro is a big help in this garden, but it plays an even more important role in Latin-Caribbean cooking. Its fragrant, strongly flavored leaves make a lasting impression in many salsas and sauces.

Patti's Picks

Petite Mixed French Marigold (*Tagetes patula*) This is an elegant, compact dwarf marigold with a mixture of orange, yellow, red, and variegated flowers. These cheerful annuals are easy-to-grow, low-maintenance plants that add visual delight to any garden.
Seed to flower 60 days
Spacing for seeds and transplants 4 per square foot
Height 6 inches

Cilantro (*Coriandrum sativum*)   Essential in Latin-Caribbean cooking—and in my special sofrito marinades (see recipes on pages 238–239)—cilantro is an annual that can be used in the kitchen as a fresh herb in many ways. After the plant flowers and develops seeds, it's referred to as coriander. Like many spices, coriander contains antioxidants, but the leaves (cilantro) have an even stronger effect.
Seed to table 55 days
Spacing for seeds 9 per square foot
Spacing for transplants One 4- to 6-inch pot per square foot
Native to Mediterranean and Southern Asia

SOFRITO GARDEN RECIPES

Latin-Caribbean cuisine is a combination of many different cultural influences—from Caribbean native peoples, Spain, and Africa, as well as East India and Asia. Ever heard of Cuban-Chinese cuisine? It's delicious. To make Latin-Caribbean dishes, you don't need any fancy cooking equipment, but if you want to prepare them the authentic way, you may want to purchase a *caldero* (a cauldron), which is simply a large pot for cooking rice. However, as long as your pot is heavy and has a tight-fitting lid, you'll be ready to go. The traditional *caldero* is made of cast iron, but a Dutch oven with a good, tight lid will serve just as well.

SOFRITO

This versatile, aromatic puree of tomatoes, peppers, onions, garlic, and cilantro is the base flavor of many Latin-Caribbean and Spanish-influenced dishes, from rice to beans to meat marinades. I invite you to try two of my family's sofrito recipes that have been modified to include veggies from the Latin-Caribbean garden.

Sofrito 1

Makes about 2 cups

There are so many variations of this recipe! You can use this simple, basic sofrito to marinate any meat, whether it is chicken, beef, or pork. It takes no time at all to whip this together—about 15 minutes—but the flavor is amazing.

1	bunch scallions, chopped
1	bunch cilantro leaves with stems
1	head organic garlic, peeled
½	cup Spanish olive oil
¼	cup vinegar
1	packet Sazón Goya

In a food processor (or blender) combine the scallions, cilantro, and garlic. Then add olive oil, vinegar, and Sazón Goya . Blend the ingredients until the consistency is just slightly chunky.

Sofrito 2

Makes about 2 cups

This sofrito is perfect to use in rice dishes, but you can also add it to sauces, soups, and stews for a quick, strong kick of Latin-Caribbean flavors. In Puerto Rico, sofrito is traditionally prepared with meat, such as bacon, salted pork, or cured ham, but here it is deliciously garden-fresh and packs a wonderful veggie wallop.

1	green bell pepper, seeded and chopped
1	red bell pepper, seeded and chopped
2	medium tomatoes, chopped
1	large bunch scallions, chopped, or 1 cup chopped white onions
1	head organic garlic, peeled
1	tsp. dried oregano
1	large bunch cilantro, leaves and stems
1	tbsp. salt
1	tbsp. black pepper

In a food processor (or blender) combine peppers, tomatoes, scallions (or onion), garlic, oregano and cilantro. Then add salt and pepper, and blend into a slightly chunky consistency.

Summer Gazpacho

Serves four

This classic, cold-soup recipe is a cinch to make and a great way to use veggies from your Latin-Caribbean garden. If you have zucchini, red peppers, and cucumbers growing in your raised beds, you can dice them up and add them to the recipe. Anything goes!

6	medium Santa Cruz Cada tomatoes, seeded
½	cup water
2	tbsp. extra-virgin olive oil
1	small bell pepper, seeded and diced
1	bunch scallions, finely chopped
2	medium garlic cloves, minced
1	small jalapeño pepper, seeded and minced
2	tbsp. sherry vinegar
2	tbsp. chopped fresh cilantro
	Salt and freshly ground black pepper, to taste

Puree half of the tomatoes with the water and oil. In a bowl, combine the puree with the rest of the ingredients. Add salt and pepper to taste and mix. Cover and refrigerate until it's time to serve. Store for up to 2 days.

Pernil (Puerto Rican Pork Shoulder)

Serves six

For my family, this roast pork is a beloved holiday tradition. Try adding it to your Thanksgiving meal for a little Caribbean flare. This recipe for pernil includes Sofrito #1 (see recipe on page 238), which is made with Sazón Goya, a seasoned salt available in almost any supermarket these days. Other ingredients in Sazón Goya include cilantro, garlic, and annatto (a natural plant extract used as red food coloring).

5	lbs. pork shoulder
8–10	garlic cloves, peeled
1	cup (or more to taste) Sofrito #1

Preheat the oven to 400°F. With a knife, stab 8 to 10 holes in the pork and rub sofrito all over it and into the holes; insert the garlic cloves into the holes. Place the roast, skin side up, in a roasting pan and cover it with aluminum foil. After 2 hours of roasting at 400°F, lower the temperature to 350°F. Roast a total of 45 minutes per pound. The roast is done when a meat thermometer inserted in the thickest part of meat reads 160°F. Uncover the roast, and bake 30 more minutes so that the skin gets crispy. Let the meat rest for at least 15 minutes before slicing. Serve with arroz con gandules (see recipe below).

Arroz con Gandules (Rice & Pigeon Peas)

Serves four to six

You can make arroz con gandules, Puerto Rico's national dish, with other beans or peas if you don't have gandules—it'll still taste great. This is my mom's recipe; it uses a little bacon instead of diced ham (a traditional ingredient), which gives the gandules a wonderful smoky taste.

2	tbsp. olive oil
½	cup Sofrito #2 (see page 239 for recipe)
2	slices bacon (optional)
1	packet low-sodium Sazón Goya
1	15-oz. can pigeon peas/gandules, drained and rinsed
½	cup whole red pepper–stuffed green olives
1	8-oz. can Goya low-sodium tomato sauce
4	cups Goya rice
4	cups water

Heat the olive oil in a 6-quart pot over high heat. When the oil is hot, fry the bacon (optional), then sauté the sofrito and bacon for 1 minute. Add the Sazón Goya, gandules, olives, and tomato sauce, and cook for 5 minutes. Rinse the rice and add it to the pot. Mix together and add the water. Bring to a boil. Cover pot with a tight-fitting lid, and reduce heat to medium low. Cook for 35–40 minutes, until the rice is soft.

Hot Pepper & Bean Salsa with Heirloom Tomatoes

Serves six

All of the fresh ingredients in this salsa are available in my garden at the same time. We have Mexican Monday at my house almost every week in the summertime, and this recipe fits right in. Be careful when you're chopping the hot peppers. Remember not to rub your eyes or skin, and wear rubber gloves if possible.

4	chili peppers, deseeded and cubed
1	cup cubed tomatoes
½	cup chopped scallions
½	cup minced fresh cilantro
2	cups cooked beans (such as red kidney beans), chilled
4	tbsp. Spanish olive oil
4	tbsp. vinegar
	Juice of one lime
	Salt and pepper, to taste

As you chop up the peppers, tomatoes, scallions, and cilantro, put them and the beans in a large bowl and mix together with the olive oil, vinegar, lime juice, and salt and pepper. Chill the salsa in the fridge. Serve with tortilla chips as a snack or as a perfect side dish or filling for tacos or burritos. This is hot stuff!

Tomato Chutney

Makes 3 cups

I learned this traditional Jamaican recipe from my friend chef Nadine Nelson, and I'm sure it will become one of your family favorites too. This chutney is a great way to put up your harvest instead of making tomato sauce. Serve this delicious relish with roasted potatoes, pork, ham, or chicken. If you like, replace the tomatoes with other vegetables such as zucchini or eggplant. You can even substitute apples or pears for the tomatoes. It's all good!

2   tbsp. olive oil

1   yellow onion, chopped

8   vine-ripened tomatoes, chopped

2   tsp. Dijon mustard

½   cup malt vinegar

½   cup brown sugar

     Sea salt and cracked black pepper, to taste

Place the oil and onion in a saucepan over medium heat and cook for 5 minutes or until the onion is tender. Add the tomatoes, mustard, vinegar, sugar, salt and pepper, and cook for 10–15 minutes or until the mixture is slightly thickened. Spoon into sterilized jars or clean containers and store in the refrigerator.

Mouth-watering Cilantro Lime Martini

Makes one large martini

You can start making this delicious garden martini the minute your cilantro is ready to be harvested. It's so refreshing!

10   fresh cilantro leaves (about a handful)

2   oz. simple syrup or raw agave nectar

2   oz. Grey Goose Vodka

     Juice of 1 lime

1   sprig of cilantro (garnish)

Fill a shaker with the cilantro leaves and simple syrup and muddle well. Add the vodka and lime juice, and fill the shaker with crushed ice. Shake vigorously for 15–30 seconds. Pour into a chilled martini glass, add a sprig of cilantro, serve immediately, and enjoy.

ABOUT THE AUTHOR

Patti Moreno is both the co-creator, with her husband Robert Patton-Spruill, and host of GardenGirltv.com, one of the top urban gardening websites in the United States, with over 15 million video views. Patti has contributed to Fine Gardening's *Grow Magazine, Organic Gardening Magazine, Farmers' Almanac, The Boston Globe, and The Huffington Post,* and is the co-host for the first season of the public television show, *Growing a Greener World*. Patti has appeared on *Today* and speaks at garden centers across the country. Patti produced and hosted the web series, Edible Gardening, available on HGTV.com. Her production company, 617Digital, produces branded video content for broadcast and the web. Patti lives in Roxbury, Massachusetts, with her husband and partner of 20 years, Rob; teenage daughter, Al; and 90-year-old grandmother-in-law, Meem.

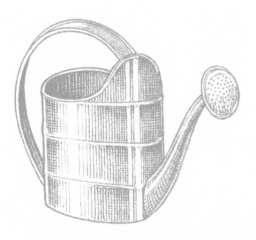

Companion Videos

This is a partial list of the free instructional videos posted on my website, **GardenGirlTV.com.** Created with the help of my gardening expert friends (including my daughter), the videos expand upon the Cuisine Gardening know-how I've provided in this book.

CHAPTER ONE
How to Check the Sun Exposure in your Garden
Know When to Water your Plants
How to Install a Drip Irrigation System
How to Install Drip Irrigation for Container Gardening
Simple Compost Bin
How to Make Compost
Composting Kitchen Scraps with a Worm Bin
Healthy Organic Soil and the Importance of pH
First Aid for a Sick Plant: Compost Tea

CHAPTER TWO
Six Ways to Win the Fight against Garden Pests
Natural Insect Control with Diatomaceous Earth

CHAPTER THREE
How to Make Seed Tape
Starting Seeds Using Toilet Paper Rolls
Simple Newspaper Pots
How to Start Vegetable Seeds
How to Start Seeds Indoors with a Hot House
Starting a Vegetable Container Indoors

CHAPTER FOUR
How to Build a Raised Bed
Vertical Gardening
How to Prepare a Raised Bed Garden for Planting
How to Sow Seeds in a Raised Bed Garden
Four Season Gardening
Spring Garden Prep Work
Making Drainage Holes in a Metal Container
Raised Beds in the City

CHAPTER FIVE
How to Freeze Culinary Herbs
How to Preserve Herbs in Ice Cubes
How to Make Fresh Mint Mojitos
How to Make a Pesto Sauce

CHAPTER SIX
How to Preserve Vegetables Using a Vacuum Sealer
How to Make Stir Fry Beef
Wasabi Vinaigrette Salad
Fall is a Perfect Time for an Asian Garden
How to Make Thai Cabbage Salad

CHAPTER SEVEN
Shaker Medicinal Herb Garden

CHAPTER EIGHT
Vertical Gardening with Cucumbers
How to Make Pickles
Cucumber Salad Fresh from the Vine

CHAPTER TEN
Planting Potatoes

CHAPTER ELEVEN
Container Gardening: How to Plant Blackberries
Garden Kid TV: Blueberries
Growing Strawberries: A Delicious Ground Cover
Tips for Growing Grapes
Growing Blueberries
How to Grow a City Vineyard
Preserving Fruit: How to Make Jam
Tips for Making Stuffed Grape Leaves

CHAPTER TWELVE
How to Plant a Three Sisters Garden
Harvesting My Three Sisters Garden
How to Make Stuffed Squash Flowers

CHAPTER THIRTEEN
Growing and Planting an Italian Kitchen Garden
Tomato Planting Tips
Heirloom Tomato Salad

CHAPTER FOURTEEN
How to Make a Cilantro Martini
How to Make Gazpacho Soup Fresh From the Garden

ACKNOWLEDGMENTS

To my Family, Friends, and Fans, thanks for your love and support.

A huge thank you to all who contributed to the success of Garden-GirlTV.com. It couldn't have happened without you: Hugh Eaton, Kim Green, Melissa Allard, Alex LoCastro, Stephen Chang, Luke Donovan, Beecher Cotton, Phil Svitek, Brad Allen Wilde, Sean Gardner, Bruce Baker, Scottie Wood, Cameron Brown, Kyle Brown, Meg Cloud, Pilot Sizwe, Cynthia VanRenterghem, Kerry VerMeulen, David Hoyt, Joe Lamp'l, Jere Gettle, John Anderes, David Vos, Carlene Hemple, Peter Koeppen, Michelle Ray, David Porter, Mel Bartholomew, Monica Dewart, Eric and Julie Harper, Scott Webster, Natasha and William Moss, Fred Dunn, John Pinkus, Nikki Crain, Leslie Halleck, Renee Bishop, Sam Jenness, Nadine Nelson, Sandra Casagrand, Mark DeAngelis, Brian Matt, Mark Highland, Edgar Milford, Rob Kelly, Christopher Hawker, Sharon Mulcahy, Lawrence Sampson, Scott Meyer, Miriam Goldberger, Bill Warner, and all of my neighbors in the Fort Hill Highland Park neighborhood in Roxbury, MA.

And another big thank you to everyone who contributed and shared their talents and experience to make this book possible—my agent, Joanne Wycoff; editors Jennifer Williams and Joseph Gonzalez; copyeditor Patricia Fogarty; and the artists and graphic designers who made this book sing: Sydney Janey, Perri DeFino, Chris Thompson, Christine Heun, and Elizabeth Mihaltse.

METRIC CONVERSION CHART

VOLUME

US	METRIC
1 teaspoon	5 ml (milliliter)
1 tablespoon	15 ml
¼ cup	60 ml
⅓ cup	80 ml
⅔ cup	160 ml
¾ cup	180 ml
1 cup	240 ml
1 pint	475 ml
1 quart	.95 liter
1 quart plus ¼ cup	1 liter
1 gallon	3.8 liters

WEIGHT

US	METRIC
1 ounce	28.3 g (grams)
4 ounces	113 g
8 ounces	227 g
12 ounces	340.2 g
16 ounces/1 pound	454 g
2 pounds	.9 kg (kilogram)
3 pounds	1.4 kg
5 pounds	2.3 kg
10 pounds	4.5 kg

TEMPERATURE*

32° F	0° C
212° F	100° C
250° F	121° C
325° F	163° C
350° F	176° C
375° F	190° C
400° F	205° C
425° F	218° C
450° F	232° C

LENGTH

US	METRIC
⅛ inch	3.2 mm (millimeter)
¼ inch	6.35 mm
½ inch	12.7 mm
¾ inch	19.05 mm
1 inch	2.54 cm (centimeter)
2 inches	5.1 cm
3 inches	7.6 cm
4 inches	10.2 cm
5 inches	12.7 cm
6 inches	15.2 cm
7 inches	17.8 cm
8 inches	20.3 cm
9 inches	22.9 cm
10 inches	25.4 cm
11 inches	27.9 cm
12 inches/1 foot	30.5 cm
2 feet	61 cm
3 feet	91 cm
4 feet	1.22 m (meter)
5 feet	1.52 m
6 feet	1.83 m
7 feet	2.13 m
8 feet	2.44 m
9 feet	2.74 m
10 feet	3.05 m
50 feet	15.24 m
100 feet	30.48 m

AREA

US	METRIC
1 square inch	6.45 sq. cm (centimeter)
1 square foot	929 sq. cm
1 square yard	.84 sq. m (meter)
1 square mile	2.59 sq. km (kilometer)

*To convert from Fahrenheit to Celsius: subtract 32, multiply by 5, then divide by 9

INDEX

Note: Page numbers in *italics* indicate recipes.